The Zen Buddhist Philosophy
of D. T. Suzuki

Bloomsbury Introductions to World Philosophies

Series Editor:
Monika Kirloskar-Steinbach

Assistant Series Editor:
Leah Kalmanson

Regional Editors:
Nader El-Bizri, James Madaio, Sarah A. Mattice, Takeshi Morisato,
Pascah Mungwini, Omar Rivera and Georgina Stewart

Bloomsbury Introductions to World Philosophies delivers primers
reflecting exciting new developments in the trajectory of world
philosophies. Instead of privileging a single philosophical approach
as the basis of comparison, the series provides a platform for diverse
philosophical perspectives to accommodate the different dimensions
of cross-cultural philosophizing. While introducing thinkers, texts
and themes emanating from different world philosophies, each book,
in an imaginative and path-breaking way, makes clear how it departs
from a conventional treatment of the subject matter.

Titles in the Series:
African Philosophy, by Pascah Mungwini
A Practical Guide to World Philosophies, by Monika Kirloskar-
Steinbach and Leah Kalmanson
Daya Krishna and Twentieth-Century Indian Philosophy,
by Daniel Raveh
Māori Philosophy, by Georgina Tuari Stewart
Philosophy of Science and the Kyoto School, by Dean Anthony Brink
Tanabe Hajime and the Kyoto School, by Takeshi Morisato
The Zen Buddhist Philosophy of D. T. Suzuki, by Rossa Ó Muireartaigh

The Zen Buddhist Philosophy of D. T. Suzuki

Strengths, Foibles, Intrigues, and Precision

Rossa Ó Muireartaigh

BLOOMSBURY ACADEMIC
LONDON · NEW YORK · OXFORD · NEW DELHI · SYDNEY

BLOOMSBURY ACADEMIC
Bloomsbury Publishing Plc
50 Bedford Square, London, WC1B 3DP, UK
1385 Broadway, New York, NY 10018, USA
29 Earlsfort Terrace, Dublin 2, Ireland

BLOOMSBURY, BLOOMSBURY ACADEMIC and the Diana logo
are trademarks of Bloomsbury Publishing Plc

First published in Great Britain 2022

Series design by Louise Dugdale
Cover image © Jelena Obradovic / Alamy Stock Vector

A catalogue record for this book is available from the British Library.

A catalog record for this book is available from the Library of Congress.

ISBN: HB: 978-1-3502-4612-6
        PB: 978-1-3502-4613-3
        ePDF: 978-1-3502-4614-0
        eBook: 978-1-3502-4615-7

Series: Bloomsbury Introductions to World Philosophies

Typeset by Integra Software Services Pvt. Ltd.
Printed and bound in Great Britain

To find out more about our authors and books visit www.bloomsbury.com
and sign up for our newsletters.

In memory of my father, Pat Murtagh (1937-2021)

Contents

Series Editor's Preface

The introductions we include in the World Philosophies series take a single thinker, theme, or text and provide a close reading of them. What defines the series is that these are likely to be people or traditions that you have not yet encountered in your study of philosophy. By choosing to include them, you broaden your understanding of ideas about the self, knowledge, and the world around us. Each book presents unexplored pathways into the study of world philosophies. Instead of privileging a single philosophical approach as the basis of comparison, each book accommodates the many different dimensions of cross-cultural philosophizing. While the choice of terms used by the individual volumes may indeed carry a local inflection, they encourage critical thinking about philosophical plurality. Each book strikes a balance between locality and globality.

The Zen Buddhist Philosophy of D.T. Suzuki: Strengths, Foibles, Intrigues, and Precision offers a novel interpretation of D.T. Suzuki's unique Zen-inflected philosophy. Endorsing a renewed engagement with this philosophy, Ó Muireartaigh offers arguments to critically evaluate—and appreciate—key aspects *of* Suzuki's work on Zen. Furthermore, *The Zen Buddhist Philosophy of D.T. Suzuki* provides translations of Suzuki's essays "Religion and Science" (1949) and "The Place of Peace in Our Heart" (1894). Both these hitherto untranslated essays complement Ó Muireartaigh's analysis of Suzuki's rich ruminations about the self, the world, and the teleological role of philosophy.

Monika Kirloskar-Steinbach

Acknowledgments

First of all, I would like to thank Morisato Takeshi and Monika Kirloskar-Steinbach for making this book possible. I am also grateful to all the editors, advisors, and anonymous reviewers at Bloomsbury for their assistance.

My knowledge of Zen and D. T. Suzuki has grown over many years, fertilized in large part by conversations and instruction from teachers, colleagues, and friends who are too many to name. But they include: John Walsh, Patrick Hubbuck, Akitoshi Nagahata, Michael Cronin, Francis Jones, Morihiko Isono, Tetsuya Isobe, Kumiko Yamada, Jim Heisig, Joe O'Leary, Wolfgang Schirmacher, Mark Daniel Cohen, Shane O'Grady, Donnacha Ó Beacháin, Declan Donnelly, Peadar Hannigan, Martin Naughton, Paul Delahunty, and Sean McKeon.

Thanks too to my family for their constant support.

I am grateful also to the students at Aichi Prefectural University and all the other universities where I have taught for helping me talk through so many of the ideas I present here. And finally, thank you to all my wonderful comrades in the European Network of Japanese Philosophy (ENOJP) who remind me each time we meet in conference that there is no greater joy than discussing and learning in good company.

Any errors in the text remain the fault of my non-existent selfhood.

Acknowledgments

Introduction

Short Biography

Daisetsu Teitaro Suzuki was born in Kanagawa Prefecture in the west of Japan in 1870.[1] His father was a doctor, and the family had been of samurai rank during the pre-modern era. Suzuki attended Ishikawa Semmon Gakko Middle School, also attended at that time by Nishida Kitaro (西田幾多郎 1870–1945), who would in due course become perhaps Japan's foremost philosopher of modern times and the effective founding figure of the Kyoto School tradition of philosophy. Suzuki and Nishida knew each other, befriended each other, and influenced and admired each other intellectually. It was an interesting time to be at school in Japan. The modern education system that would help make the nation an industrial giant in a few decades time was taking firm root. But many of the old teachers with their old ways and old texts still lingered and a certain Meiji *ostalgie* (to coin a phrase)—an affection for the pre-modern and pre-Westernized Japan of a few decades previous—still pervaded. Suzuki's own language education reflects this liminality. He studied English and soon got work teaching the language after leaving school, but one of his first pieces of writing was in old Chinese, a language the youth of Japan were to soon lose access to (similar to the demise of Latin in schools in the West in the late twentieth century).[2]

By early adulthood Suzuki was in Tokyo attending Tokyo University as an auditing student taking classes in American literature. His next foray into Zen practice was the Engakuji Temple in Kamakura, many miles south of Tokyo to which Suzuki used to walk. Engakuji at this time was run by Imakita Kōsen (今北 洪川1816–1892) and Shaku Soyen (釈

宗演 1860–1919, sometimes spelled "Soen"). The pair were innovative and open-minded rōshi (Zen masters), well suited to the modern times. Kōsen came from a Confucianist background and had converted to Zen Buddhism in youth. He had written in the late Edo period texts that explained Zen in terms of Confucianism, arguing how Zen can be found in alternate and seemingly rival systems of thought.[3] It was an ecumenicalism that would in many ways adumbrate Suzuki's later efforts. Shaku Soyen was the epitome of a new style of modernized Zen Buddhism. He had attended modern university and had travelled to Sri Lanka to study pre-Mahāyāna Buddhism (something hitherto impossible for Japanese people living in the period of national seclusion). Kōsen and Soyen were pivotal in transforming Zen into something more accessible to the modern people by opening their temple to lay Zen practice and in facilitating, in particular in the case of Soyen, intellectual explanations of Zen in a way that could be respected by a modern readership.[4]

In 1896, Suzuki published his book *Shinshūkyōron* (『新宗教論』 [New Interpretation of Religion]), which expressed many of the core ideas Suzuki had about religion and which he would maintain throughout his life, the major one being that religions need to not only make themselves more scientifically respectable but also appreciate that deep within themselves they express an unchanging truth that science will never be able to grasp.[5] Suzuki's big break came when he was sent to the United States to work with Paul Carus (1852–1919), a German-American philosopher. Soyen had met Carus at the World Parliament of Religions, an event held in Chicago in 1893 that brought many leaders of the major world religions together.[6] Soyen and Carus found they had a lot in common intellectually and this marked a new development for Zen Buddhism which would now be given a far more secular and philosophically respected spin in the wider United States and Western society. Paul Carus ran the Open Court Press, an eclectic philosophy publishing company, from a house in La Salle, Illinois. This is where Suzuki worked, involved in every aspect of the physical labors of publishing and printing. He also worked with Carus on various translations of texts from ancient Chinese into modern

English, including a rhyming version of the Tao-Te-Ching translated as *The Canon of Reason and Virtue*.[7] Suzuki's books and articles in English during this period include introductions to ancient Chinese philosophy and Mahāyāna Buddhism.[8] What is particularly noteworthy is Suzuki's liberal use of Western philosophical terminology in his descriptions of these other traditions. Confucius is "positivist" and Chwang-tze (Zhuangzi) is a "transcendentalist." While his book *Outlines of Mahayana Buddhism* seeks to undo some of the misunderstandings that were current at the time regarding Buddhism, in particular the accusation that it espouses nihilism, his explanations of Buddhist concepts are devoid of the rhetorical flourishes, excitable descriptions, and anti-rational, or rather arational assertions that are to be found in so much of his later work on Zen. During this time, Suzuki was influenced by Carus to the extent that he shared with Carus a pluralist view of religions and openness to other traditions to express the same truths. But he did not fully share all aspects of Carus's (monist) philosophy and it would not be correct to identify him as his protégé.[9]

Suzuki returned to Japan the long way, stopping in Europe to translate into Japanese some works of the mystic Emmanuel Swedenborg, who would remain another influence in Suzuki's intellectual development. He settled in Tokyo but later moved to Kyoto where he taught at Otani University while continuing to write in Japanese and English on Zen Buddhism, including the well-received three volume *Essays in Zen Buddhism* and *Zen Buddhism and Its Influence on Japanese Culture*. He put his experience publishing and printing with Carus in Illinois to good use producing the *Eastern Buddhist Journal* over many years. During his time at Otani University he translated the Laṅkāvatāra Sutra from Sanskrit into both Japanese and English, a project that marked him as a much accomplished scholar and philologist. By the 1920s and 1930s, Suzuki would have been quite well known to a small number of Western intellectuals, including, for example W.B. Yeats who subscribed to the *Eastern Buddhist Journal*.[10] Suzuki was in most respects the foremost commentator on matters Zen in the west. Indeed, those wanting to know more about not only Zen but Buddhism, Japan, and Asian culture in general found Suzuki to be a convenient gateway. Suzuki married the American Beatrice Erskine Lane and they had a son named Alan.

By the time the Second World War broke out, Suzuki was in his sixties and now widowed and retired, and living at Engakuji in Kamakura, where it had all started for him many decades earlier. While not completely outspoken about the issue, he did voice criticism of Japan's decision to enter the war and how the war was being conducted. During the war he wrote in Japanese the book *Nihontekireisei* (『日本的霊性』 [Japanese Spirituality], 1944)[11] in which he explored the history of Pure Land Buddhism in Japan, which allowed him to create new concepts to describe the closeness between religion, consciousness, and lives lived in simple but absolute faith. The book is controversial because it does contain uncritically simplistic and unreflectively absolute notions of ethnic identities. Its tone is twee patriotism. This would be forgivable but for the time it was written in (the early 1940s), when Japan was overdosing on nationalism and large chunks of the world's population were suffering the resultant insanity. It could be argued that the book is a private protest against an aggressive militarist style of nationalism instead of which Suzuki was proposing a style of nationalism that was peaceful and humble, and would do nothing worse to neighboring countries other than religiously inspire them. Either way, the book suggests Suzuki's reaction to the war was one of withdrawal rather than active collaboration or resistance.

Richard DeMartino relates how, when stationed in Tokyo at the end of the War working for the Tokyo War Trials, he along with Philip Kapleau sought out Suzuki at his Engakuji refuge, as did Christmas Humphreys, who was also working for the Tokyo Tribunal. No doubt these people saw Suzuki as a revered master of the nicer and more ancient wisdom Japan still had to offer. Certainly, they felt Suzuki had no case to answer for any wartime collaboration.[12] A few short years later and Suzuki's career once again rocketed forward when he took up a teaching post at Columbia University in New York at the very moment his writings and Zen in general were finding a new audience among the generation of Beats.

This was a period that has been dubbed the "Zen boom" when Suzuki's esoteric writings and views were becoming more and more featured in the mainstream press and "Zen" was becoming a household word.[13] Suzuki, at this stage in his life an elderly conservative, was not completely happy with this popularization and the antics of the Beat rebels. But either way, Suzuki was well respected among newer networks of intellectuals. During this period, for example, he befriended Eric Fromm, as we shall see, and maintained a dialogue of a sort with Christian philosopher Thomas Merton. All the while he was continuing to produce books in English and Japanese on Zen and Buddhism in general. In Japan, Suzuki had, as noted, been a friend of Nishida Kitaro, the de facto founding father of the Kyoto School of Philosophy. But now Suzuki himself was a figure of inspiration for many in the next generation of Kyoto School philosophers. Certainly Nishitani Keiji (西谷 啓治 1900–1990), Hisamatsu Shin'ichi (久松 真一 1889–1980), Masao Abe (阿部 正雄 1915–2006), and Ueda Shizuteru (上田 閑照 1926–2019) admired him and learned from him. Tanabe Hajime (田辺 元 1885–1962) was less inspired, feeling irritated by Suzuki's anti-philosophy Zen posturing.

Suzuki finally passed away at the age of 95 in 1965. The journal he had founded, the *Eastern Buddhist Journal*, produced a special obituary edition upon the occasion of his death in which intellectuals, academics, and others from the world over wrote testimonies to the personal warmth, natural kindness, intellectual power, and spiritual profundity of Suzuki.[14] We can disagree with many of his ideas and balk at the odd wild comment he made in his very long writing and speaking career, but the consensus from those who knew him first hand is that he was fundamentally a good person.

Two Births of Buddha Wisdom

Buddhism traditionally offers two stories concerning the younger days of Siddhattha Gotama, the historical Buddha.[15] One describes the birth of Buddha in miraculous terms. According to this account, the

Buddha emerged from his mother out of her armpit and immediately stood up and proudly declared, "above and below the earth I alone am the honored one." The other story goes that Buddha was a much more modest prince who lived a very sheltered and naïve life but who one day upon seeing people suffering began to question why life and existence is full of sorrow and death. This led him to experiencing an awakening while meditating under a *bodhi* tree. The two stories make for an obvious contrast. The first story suggests that the Buddha had innately superior wisdom and powers of which he was born aware of. The second story expresses a more human Buddha who had to go through his own searching and learning to obtain enlightenment.

D. T. Suzuki's status as a sage of Zen has similarly two versions. For many, Suzuki was innately in every way a man of Zen with a core mystical depth of character who could calmly face the vicissitudes of life with a grace and equanimity neurotic Westerners were wise to learn from. Suzuki never encouraged such hero-worship but his efforts to resist it only created more of it in a *Life of Brian* style dynamic where messiah denials generate messiah status. But the fact is that Suzuki, and he never hid this, had to learn Zen and struggle for enlightenment the same as anyone else. Suzuki shares a tale of the first time he ever visited a Zen temple:

> I decided to visit a Zen master, Setsumon Rōshi, who lived in a temple called Kokutaiji near Takaoka in the province of Etchū ... I arrived without any introduction, but the monks were quite willing to take me in. They told me the Rōshi was away, but that I could do zazen in a room in the temple if I liked. They told me how to sit and how to breathe and then left me alone in a little room telling me to go on like that. After a day or two of this the Rōshi came back and I was taken to see him. Of course, at that time I really knew nothing of Zen and had no idea of the correct etiquette in *sanzen*. I was just told to come and see the Rōshi, so I went, holding my copy of the *Orategama*. Most of the *Orategama* is written in fairly easy language, but there are some difficult Zen terms in it which I could not understand, so I asked the Rōshi the meaning of these words. He turned on me angrily and said,

"Why do you ask me a stupid question like that?" I was sent back to my room without any instruction and told simply to go on sitting cross-legged.[16]

In many ways, Suzuki's life project and achievement was to rise to the role of a Zen authority and challenge and chastise the West for its excessive intellectualism and rationalizations, just as he had been chastised himself all those years ago in a remote temple in Etchū (Toyama Prefecture). In doing so, he forced the west to take Zen and Buddhism seriously, to see it as presenting its own unique paradigm and philosophy that could never be easily reduced to traditional Western philosophical categories. With Suzuki's forceful hectoring, Zen shocked the mid- to late-twentieth-century world and made many of the West's foremost intellectuals scramble to understand it anew.

Suzuki and Philosophy

Suzuki was a great intellectual multi-tasker. He was a translator who produced contemporary English and Japanese versions of ancient Chinese, Sanskrit, and Japanese texts. He was a Zen historian who studied primary sources, including from the Dun Huang caves, to shed new light on the development of Zen thinking in Ancient China. He was a religious scholar who sought new understandings and interpretations of Buddhist scripture. He was a preacher and apologist promoting Zen and Buddhism to English speakers in memorable and inspiring books and essays. He was an interpreter of Japanese culture, explaining its arts and ways to faraway readers in English. He was a social commentator penning articles bemoaning the wows of the modern youth and society. And he was a philosopher. This book aims to shed light on this philosophical work and to do so, it is necessary to ignore or downplay all the other intellectual work he engaged in. Furthermore, Suzuki wrote philosophically about other branches of Buddhism in addition to Zen, in particular Pure Land and, to a lesser extent, Kegon. Again, this book will stick mostly to the Zen writings.

One of the problems with writing a book on Suzuki's philosophy of Zen is the fact that Suzuki long claimed that Zen has no philosophy and if we can garner a philosophy out of his descriptions of Zen then we must have misunderstood Zen. Zen is about direct experience, the experience of the here and now, an experience that cannot be mediated, as in represented by any other secondary or derivative experience. Zen is as different from philosophy as the letters "w," "i," "n," and "e" are from the sensation you get when you sip a glass of wine. Philosophy works with language always. It interprets our experiences through ideas which are represented by concepts which are formulated into words. The words stand at the long end of a chain of mediation between actual experience, abstract ideas, coherent concepts, and words on a page. Zen, the absolute and uncompromising awareness of direct experience, cannot ever be dragged into life-sucking scrolls of withering and desiccating philosophizing.

But there is a simple answer to this. To claim that Zen has no philosophy is itself a philosophical claim. The idea that the word "Zen" and everything we have to *say* about Zen represent a direct experience that cannot be mediated is, itself, a philosophical assertion. If not then I should be allowed to replace the word "Zen" with any other word I care to choose and make the same claim. For example, I can say that "Fineaism" is a direct experience that cannot be mediated and hence philosophically justified. I can claim myself to be a Fineaist master, write books about Fineaist influences in art and culture, and set up tax-exempt Fineaist institutions. But to distinguish "Zen," a living truth, religion, belief, and system of values, from "Fineaism" (a word I just made up) takes philosophy. Of course, there is a distinction to be made between Zen as an experience and everything we have to say about that experience. But this is a distinction that can be made between any philosophy and the very reality and experiences that it is trying to explain and justify. For instance, Kant's idea about space and time being intuitions is, of course, completely different from my experience right now of space and time which is an experience that is just there, regardless of whatever Kant wrote or didn't write. In many ways what Suzuki is claiming—that direct experience and philosophy are two separate things—is actually a frivolous insight. That what represents and what is represented are two separate things is something almost everyone knows from a very early age (maybe even as far back as when we are toddlers) and is something that philosophy has long been aware of, a case in point being Plato's hatred of poets and their mediating musings.

But not only is it a frivolous claim it is also, potentially, a dangerous claim, a religious fundamentalist claim. Now, Suzuki was, of course, never ever guilty of fanaticism. His political and social views (including during the Second World War) always tended to be bland and non-contentious. But the point still stands. If you declare your beliefs to be beyond the realm of philosophical discussion you are claiming privileges that an open society should not grant you. You are entitled to your own private direct experiences but any truth claims about the nature of the world or any moral insights about how to construct the good society that you gain from that direct experience will have to be justified and held up to scrutiny by the wider community.

In point of fact, Suzuki's rejection of philosophy was always tempered and qualified. While he was dismissive of philosophy ever being capable of offering a valid representation of Zen, he also recognized the fact that philosophy is unavoidable, acknowledging that "the conceptualization of Zen is inevitable: Zen must have its philosophy. The only caution is not to identify Zen with a system of philosophy, for Zen is infinitely more than that."[17] Society will always demand philosophy even from, indeed, especially from the absolutely enlightened. At the end of the day, the claim that Zen does not have a philosophy is denied by the very fact that Zen has always been explained philosophically by Suzuki and others. As Henry Rosemont argues, "In their attempts to articulate the beliefs of the [Zen] masters, to assert that those beliefs are true, and to defend them, the Zen commentators offer prima facie evidence that they themselves, at least, are holding those beliefs philosophically."[18]

Suzuki's Core Philosophical Ideas

What core ideas formed the grand pillars of Suzuki's philosophy? Nishitani Keiji looked for a succinct outline of Suzuki's philosophy. The first thing he pointed out was how consistent Suzuki was in his core ideas which he developed early and sustained throughout his career.

> Included in the eighteenth volume of Daisetz Suzuki's Complete Works are two rather unique writings, *Various Problems of Zen* and *The Primary Meaning of Zen*. The former was published in 1941 with the following included in the preface: "This is a collection of slightly scholarly writings about Zen which I wrote over the past ten years." The latter was published in 1914 and is a very early piece. Between these two writings is a period of almost thirty years, and yet there are essential features common to both.[19]

Nishitani then set out to describe what the essential features of Suzuki's philosophy were:

> First of all, he emphasized in both works that the primary meaning or essence of Zen cannot be realized without the actual experience, without one's own living fact of real mastery, of real Awakening. He took a psychological approach to elucidate this. Secondly, he rejected all logic, considered science and also philosophy as the standpoint of discriminating intellect and, concerning the primary meaning of Zen, he emphasized that religion and philosophy are completely unrelated to each other. Thirdly, he showed that Zen is not just Buddhism but the consummation of all religion, and that living religious faiths such as the (Pure Land) *nembutsu* and also Christianity culminate in the Zen Awakening, provided they are thoroughgoing.[20]

We can list these three core ideas as roughly *phenomenological empiricism*, *arationalism*, and *Zen universalism*. Each of the core ideas (happily) dovetail smoothly with the notions of *self*, *knowledge*, and *world* which form the titles for the chapters of this book. *Phenomenological empiricism*, as I define it, is the idea that the starting point for our truths is the truths we experience for ourselves (as opposed to truths, for instance, we hear about, read about, or have taught to us). What we experience, we experience directly in the here and now, and this experience of the here and now challenges the notion of a coherent self in space and time standing distinct from the world. *Arationality* is the insight that our direct experience of the world in the here and now can only be described in non-rational or irrational terms. This is an explicit rejection of the idea that truth can be known through logical and rational enquiry since such enquiries are partial and distorting. *Zen universality* is the idea that this direct experience of the here and now, the essence of Zen, is not specific to Zen Buddhism, that is, the actual living religion of Zen that emerged in history, but can be experienced by anyone regardless of creed.

Each of these ideas generates its own problems. If there is no self then who is doing the experiencing? When we declare our knowledge to be irrational are we not dangerously making mere assumptions and assertions based on our own inner feelings and values which can fall prey to the prejudice and narcissisms of our more ugly nature? And finally, and most controversially, if Zen is to be found in all religions why is there then a Zen Buddhist religion? Is Zen Buddhism the true religion of which all other religions are bad copies? Or is Zen Buddhism contradicting itself by being a particular religion while confusingly claiming to be a universal true experience not specific to any religion?

Suzuki Reputation as Philosopher

Suzuki's status as a philosopher has been discussed over the years. Hiroshi Sakamoto has argued that he was "... in broader and indeed unique sense, a philosopher not only in the bent of his mind but also in the attitude of his lifelong scholarly activities."[21] Japanese philosopher Shimomura Torataro also argues for recognition of Suzuki's importance as a philosopher.[22] Zen historian Heinrich Dumoulin was more skeptical arguing that Suzuki's "affection for philosophy was that of 'a would-be philosopher.'"[23] Thomas Kasulis points out that Suzuki's anti-philosophical philosophizing did not suit the rational language-respecting analytical philosophical tradition that was strong at the time he was working in the English-speaking world. However, Kasulis does acknowledge that "... there were little pockets of philosophical interest (especially among those in the Continental tradition) that did not follow the pattern of the mainstream. Heidegger himself was impressed by Suzuki in their personal encounters."[24] Indeed, William Barrett tells us the following tale: "A German friend of Heidegger told me that one day when he visited Heidegger he found him reading one of Suzuki's books; 'If I understand this man correctly,' Heidegger remarked, 'this is what I have been trying to say in all my writings.'"[25] So what were the words that Suzuki took from right out of Heidegger's mouth? I hope the next few chapters will capture some of them.

1

Self

Introduction

D. T. Suzuki's view of the self follows the traditional Mahāyāna Buddhist[1] approach, which is to assert the ultimate non-existence of the self and in so doing offer a more complicated picture of our everyday experiences of the world through time. This explanation does not deny our actual everyday experiences of selfhood (that inner feeling that you exist) but argues that these experiences, if not understood properly, lead to the false notion that you have a coherent, unchanging, inner core self that moves around in a world that is completely external and distinct from it. It is this idea of an *essentialized* self acting in a world that is *out there* that Suzuki and Mahāyāna Buddhism attack.

To appreciate the full force of Suzuki and Zen's view of the self, it is probably best to start with the conventional view of the self against which Zen makes its argument. The power of the Zen view of the self is that it can deal with the contradictions and mysteries that arise when our own selfhood and consciousness is fully explored and considered. As such, I will spend the next few sections discussing the traditional philosophical problems that haunt considerations of the self and consciousness before presenting how Suzuki's alternative viewpoint works to reconfigure these apparent "problems" of the self as, in fact, manifestations and confirmations of the Zen philosophy of the mind, self, and consciousness.

The Problem of One's Self

We experience the world through our own self-conscious selfhood. We think therefore we are. Only you experience the world as you. Even God (as God) does not have your experiences of selfhood. You see the world through one pair of eyes and the world out there does not deny you exist. You can bang against random objects and feel the pain, you can watch animals bound away in fear when you approach, and you can see other humans seeing you. It is impossible to ignore that you are in the world as another moving animate object. Who could ever deny this? And yet, with some reflection, the existence of the self cannot be so easily assumed. There are problems with the self.

To have a self, one needs a coherent consciousness. This is the difference between having a self and being just another object in the world. However, the problem with consciousness is that it is not at all coherent. We do not remember when we first became a self. Our earliest memories are vague events and do not give us any idea of our starting point in time. Similarly, our consciousness does tend to come and go even as we are living in the world. We sleep, we lose focus, our memories fade. All this points to the fact that selfhood is not coherent through time. It is not a lump of material existing from one moment to the next in space. To liken it to ripples in the ocean is a better metaphor, but here too the comparison to phenomena in nature is misleading. Waves in an ocean, as we see them, arise as part of the linear movement of mechanical cause and effect. We can sit with a stopwatch and time a wave coming and going. Thoughts and sensations in the mind do not have the same connection with time. A conscious experience is always in the now. It cannot be timed. To time a conscious experience would be to tangle oneself in the most excruciating webs of self-reflection and infinite regresses. I can time a wave because I, a detached observer, can see it rippling out there. To time my thoughts would immediately mean I have lost my thoughts. I would be timing something that is not there anymore. The thought that a thought has finished is a different thought to the thought that has finished.

To say, then, that consciousness takes place in the now, and not in linear time, is to say that notions of selfhood are attached to something—the consciousness—that does not actually exist in time. The self, in terms of linear time, never happens. But not only is the self never happening (the problem of self in time), it is also nowhere happening. There is a problem of the self in space. Again, this problem arises from the fact that we ascribe the existence of the self to the existence of a consciousness in the material world with all the consistency and coherence we assume any material object will have. If I want to see if a material object exists, I merely have to locate it in the physical world. The problem here is that there is no actual material place or point at which consciousness can be located "physically." We do know that there are parts of the body, i.e., the brain and neurological system, which are the site of consciousness since consciousness does not operate without these. But neurons are not consciousness. As has been famously pointed out by Leibniz and others, if we were to expand the size of a brain to that of a giant machine or mill, and could walk around it, we would still not be able to see the thoughts, ideas, sensations, and memories that run through the mind.[2]

But this is not to say that consciousness is not connected to the brain. Indeed, we know from science that consciousness, and in turn the self, can be physically manipulated and changed. With the modern tools of neuroscience, or even just a bottle of whiskey, we can demonstrate an essential point in the philosophy of the mind: that our coherent selfhood undergirded by a continuous consciousness with an inherent personality can radically alter when tampered with by external physical stimuli. However, fascinating and all as these experiments with the brain are, they still do not actually physically locate consciousness. They merely locate those things that can affect consciousness second hand. The problem is that physical stimuli on the brain, and the tools of science that observe them, are out there in the material world. They are part of the third-person experience of the world, that which is detached from us and can be observed by us as something different to us. But consciousness is an "I" experience. Again, just as it is impossible to time conscious experience, it is also impossible to see it. To see it would mean to see it as a third-person experience, not as an "I" experience. To see consciousness as an "I" experience means that you are actually that experience, you are doing the seeing, you are the eyes which sees, which means that you cannot see it. An eye never sees itself. In a word, consciousness is nowhere. It cannot be located in material nature. Only its shadow, the third-person view of consciousness can be observed, which must never be confused for the first-person sight of consciousness.

Problems of consciousness are problems of the self. The consciousness being nowhere and never there makes the self, itself, something that is nowhere and never there. But there is an even further complication, and that is the issue of our freewill. We experience the self as a free-willing agent. We must constantly make decisions and never have the luxury of having the cosmos make our decisions for us. Even if we decide to relinquish our freewill, become completely still and immobile, do nothing and just blow in the wind, we have still *decided* to do this and so are not really giving up freewill. Freewill is not a choice. We are cursed with it. And yet to argue for freewill is to argue for the existence of a self that is not subject to the laws of cause and effect. A rock rolling down a hill does not decide to roll down that hill. It is pushed and pulled down by the forces of nature. My decision to roll a rock down a hill cannot be so automatic. I have to decide: push or don't push. I could close my eyes and pray to the cosmos to make my mind up for me but this is just shoving the freewill problem onto other actions. The point is, the universe does not have control over my selfhood. I am a chink in the chain of cause and effect. A cosmic error.

Science and social science are able to pinpoint those aspects of the wider world which will influence our decisions more than others. It is possible to manipulate the decision-making of another. But this is not the point, for no matter how much our decisions may be manipulated we are still experiencing ourselves as making them. When I decide to push a rock down a hill I may be acting due to a multitude of external stimuli, influences, and controls. Whether I push the rock or not may depend upon my age, my social status (some people just never push rocks down hills), or strange internal subconscious urges. But my need to make the decision to push the rock or not push the rock never goes away whether I like it or not, no matter the social and psychological contexts.

To summarize: We know we have a self because we experience it. But it is a mystery how nature can produce this self. In turn the self cannot be located anywhere in nature, and does not exist as a coherent unit. Furthermore, the self has the unusual ability to break the laws of nature by making decisions outside of the automatic, mechanical flow of the universe. In other words, the self comes from nowhere, the self is nowhere, the self is nothing, and the self is bound to nothing. For D. T. Suzuki, though, these are not problems but solutions. As Suzuki states:

> Thus, as the Self moves from zero to infinity and from infinity to zero, it is in no way an object of scientific studies. As it is absolute subjectivity, it eludes all our efforts to locate it at any objectively definable spot. As it is so elusive and cannot be taken hold of, we cannot experiment with it in any scientific way. We cannot entrap it by any objectively constructed media. With all scientific talents this can never be performed, because it is not in the nature of things within their sphere of operation. The Self when properly adjusted knows how to discover itself without going through the process of objectification.[3]

Self in the Philosophy of Buddhism

How does Buddhist philosophy square the self with the cosmological circle? One way it does so is by embracing (as expostulated in the *Lankāvatāra Sutra*[4]) the concept of "no-birth" and rejecting the idea of cause and effect entirely in the world. To quote the Sutra (as translated by Suzuki):

> Nothing is born; being is not, non-being is not, nowhere is being -and-non-being; except that where there is a system, there is the rising of things and their dissolution. It is only in accordance with general convention that a chain of mutual dependence is talked of; birth has no sense when the chain of dependence is severed.[5]

This makes sense when we considered that all that happens at one moment is happening at the same time. Hence nothing is *really* causing anything else. The chain of mutual dependence through linear time that we see masks the fact that absolutely all phenomena arise together in a state of absolute codependence. When a rock rolls down a hill nothing has caused this. Gravity does not pull it. The hill does not push it. The hill is just there, as is the force of gravity. If we seek causes for such events, we run into absurdities as each cause presumes a prior one. If we say that the slope of the hill causes the rock to roll, we must also say that the movements of the Earth's tectonic plates, which caused the hill to slope, also caused the rock to roll. But tectonic features of the planet were caused by the positioning of the Earth at the distance it is from the Sun. When we try to include every cause we will end up having to describe absolutely everything that has ever happened up until the moment the rock rolls down the hill. In other words, everything causes everything. Everything is the result of everything. Everything happens with everything else. It all arises codependently.

But what about free-willing humans? What if a human pushes the rock down the hill? Can we not say that this is the cause of the rock rolling? Only if you think that humans are not part of nature, that humans are in the realm of the divine, that which can move without a mover. But if we see us mortal humans as part of this world, then we must see humans, too, as part of the co-dependent arising of the cosmos. When I push that rock down the hill, biological evolution (which gives me the arms to push) and the movement of tectonic plates (which ensured both that organic life could evolve, and that the hill doth slope) are also causing it. We are back to the same conclusions. Everything causes me to push the rock. So synchronized is the cosmos that at the moment I push the rock I am not even really pushing it all, I am merely moving as the rock moves.

We can talk, of course, about necessary causes versus contingent causes. If I was not there the rock would not roll. I am necessary. The hill is contingent since it alone does not cause the rock to roll. But the necessary versus contingent distinction is a fiction. A necessary fiction as we would not be able to describe our world without it. But in the end both I and the hill need to exist together for the rock to roll. To distinguish the two is to carve out a story that ignores the effectively indescribable cosmic wholistic and holistic narration where hill, rock, and I move as one.

Similarly, the self is a necessary fiction.[6] As Suzuki writes, "Individuality is merely an aspect of existence; in thought we separate one individual from another and in reality too we all seem to be distinct and separable. But when we reflect on the question more closely we find that individuality is a fiction, for we cannot fix its limits, we cannot ascertain its extent and boundaries, they become mutually merged without leaving any indelible marks between so-called individuals."[7] We usually think our lives are lived upon a stage full of props and other players, upon which we move, consciously acting out the drama of our lives. But really our lives are in a movie that has been already made, inscribed on a roll of celluloid, one frame moving to the next with nothing actually moving, merely each photographed instance simply looking different to the one prior. Who is watching this movie of the cosmos that has already been made and in which you are moved? Is it God? No, that is not the Buddhist answer. The Buddhist answer is "you." You are watching the movie of the cosmos that has already been made. To have assigned this role to a trans-historical God would have been to suppose two separate beings. But Buddhism will constantly emphasize non-duality, that is, the idea that there ultimately is never two. The cosmos of co-dependent arising is self-contained and there is nothing outside except your experience of it.[8]

However, this may seem to be making the argument that there are two "you-s." There is the "you" in nature (as in, the you acting in the "movie," to continue with my metaphor) which is haunted by the curse of decision-making it can never escape. This is the hassled everyday "you" that does not feel itself at all to be part of a great harmonious co-dependently arising cosmos. And then there is the "you" that is detached, watching it all flow. Two "you-s": the you that is another object of nature and the you (or "I") that stands outside of the push and pull of nature. But, we must remember, Buddhist psychology is never dualistic, and these two "you-s," two minds, two consciousnesses, will always have to be remerged into one in any final description. And so, as with any psychological theorizing, it is with metaphors that we must precede.

In *The Awakening of Faith*, a fundamental Mahāyāna text ascribed to Aśvaghoṣa,[9] translated by D. T. Suzuki at the turn of the twentieth century, we read the following neat metaphor (or simile to be exact):

> Though all modes of consciousness and mentation are mere products of ignorance, ignorance in its ultimate nature is identical and not-identical with enlightenment *a priori*; and therefore ignorance in one sense is destructible, while in the other sense it is indestructible. This may be illustrated by [the simile of] the water and the waves which are stirred up in the ocean. Here the water can be said to be identical [in one sense] and not-identical [in the other sense] with the waves. The waves are stirred up by the wind, but the water remains the same." [square brackets in the original][10]

What is being illustrated here is that a wave, a disturbance, is something that comes and goes, while the water remains the same. So too, the mind is disturbed by our thoughts and concerns, which can give rise to the idea that it is these individual thoughts and concerns that are the mind when really the mind is something that is just there, like water, irreducible to surface and secondary manifestations. These disturbances on the water are likened to the "defilement" of the mind, which, as Suzuki explains, "is the product of the evolution of the *ālaya-vijnâna*."

Ālaya-vijnâna itself is an intriguing metaphor, meaning literally "storehouse consciousness,"[11] although Suzuki uses the translation "all-conserving mind." What is stored in the *ālaya-vijnâna*? The answer is *bīja*, or "seed-forms." When unleashed they become the little bitty bits of consciousness. They blow out from the storehouse, clustering into fake individualized ego consciousnesses. We need to gather them back into where they originally belonged, back into the great storehouse.[12] Note how these metaphors (and similes) always imply that the two minds, two consciousnesses, two "you-s" are not really two but something that is one but that has rippled out a bit from its primordial purity. What these metaphors are suggesting is that our consciousness, as we experience it, has another layer *below* it. In effect, there is always a consciousness within and of our consciousness. There is another you that is seeing you. This other layer neither must be confused with simply being self-aware of your own thinking, thinking about the fact that you are thinking and so on, nor must be confused with the unconscious of modern psychology and psychoanalysis. (Suzuki is clear about this is his book *Zen Buddhism and Psychoanalysis.*[13]) Such thoughts and consciousnesses are all confined within your own individual mind, the same mind that gives you the apparatus to assume your own selfhood. This consciousness of consciousness comes from a much deeper source that is not boxed within your individual existence. This extra layer of consciousness upholds a no-self qua non-dualistic selfhood in that the apparent distinction between the self and the rest of the world upon which it looks out on has been undercut by a deeper consciousness that pre-exists such distinctions. This deeper consciousness provides for the consciousness of distinction but because it is the source of these distinctions it is also the source for the deeper wisdom that such distinctions are not as real as the unaware distracted mind may believe.

However, the danger now is that we have dismissed our world as delusion, our most cherished thoughts and loves as fantasy, and are marching on a nihilistic crusade to embrace a wisdom which may be profound but is utterly empty lacking everything we have known. This is, of course, not the point of Buddhism. We need to go back to our non-dualizing metaphors of water and waves, and a great storehouse of consciousness full of seed-"bytes" and drive the analogies further. The waves on the water and the seeds blowing out from the storehouse both arise from disturbance. But to fully attain full delivery from these disturbances, it is not enough to annihilate the wave-causing wind, or to put all the seeds back into the storehouse. We must go one step further to fully attain authentic non-duality. And that is to annihilate all. No water, no waves, no storehouse, no seeds.[14] When this happens you do not get a negative nothing, as in everything is now gone. Instead you get the pure absolute nothing from which everything is still there.

This wisdom of (and from) a deeper consciousness embedded in pure emptiness into which we can awake can be practically demonstrated, for example, in the arts of Zen, such as kendo (archery), where, to use my earlier analogy, you can see yourself as part of the greater cosmic movie, and just watch the flow of the movie from without rather than flustering and floundering like screen actors within the frame. Don't shoot at the target. Just watch as the target gets shot at. As Suzuki says in his Foreword to Eugen Herrigel's *Zen in the Art of Archery*, "In the case of archery, the hitter and the hit are no longer two opposing objects, but are one reality."[15] But as well as making one a rather dashing ace with a bow and arrow, this non-self view of the self also manages to dissolve the problems of consciousness that have taxed the brains (or is it minds?) of philosophers of the mind for centuries.

Self in Emptiness

The concept of non-self implies that there are two minds/selves/consciousnesses that are one because all is nothingness. To tie this together, perhaps we should listen, with Suzuki, to the exhortations of the old Zen masters. This will help us understand that this sense of the conscious self within us is not a part of the linear process of time nor localizable in space nor attachable to the chain of cause and effect.

The sixth Patriarch of Zen, Hui Neng [Japanese: Eno] (638–713) asked, "What was your original face you had before you were born of your own parents?"[16] A similar question from the Zen literature is "Before my parents gave birth to me, where is my nose?"[17] These questions are similar to the one we must all have ponder at some time: "What would I be like if my parents had never met?" The breezy answer is to say that you would be nothing, you would not be here. But the idea of you not being here is just as mysterious as the idea of you being here. If you were not to be here where would the cosmos exist? Sure, materialism will have its assured answer: it would still exist, *out* there, but just with you not *in* it. Yet the answer depends on describing, once again, consciousness in "third person" terms. Could the "I" experience really be an accident of nature, or was your existence an absolute necessity, your face something that was originally ordained to happen? The Zen answer would be to stop thinking the question in terms of linear time. As Suzuki explains it:

> When the monk asks about his "nose" before his coming into this world or sense and intellect, the master retorts by referring to the monk's actual presence, to his "as-he-is-ness." From the relative point of view this answer is no answer; it does not locate the monk's "nose" … The point that I am trying to make is that Zen starts where time has not come to itself; that is to say, where timelessness has not negated itself so as to have a dichotomy of subject-object, Man-Nature, God-world. This is the abode of what I call "pure subjectivity."[18]

Again, the mystery of the "I" experience of consciousness, as discussed above, is its disconnect with linear time. But this should not be seen as a riddle to be solved but as the very nature of consciousness, that it is something beyond time, existing in the absolute now, irrelevant to the accidents of nature's evolution, and should be understood to be such.

As with time, as with space. A non-self is a nowhere self. Lin-chi (Rinzai), the great Tang period Zen master once delivered a sermon, saying: "Over a mass of reddish flesh there sits a true man who has no title; he is all the time coming in and out from your sense-organs. If you have not yet testified to the fact, Look! Look!"[19] This "true man who has no title" is this "I" experience that cannot be reduced to material nature. You are not your physical body (although you are *not* not your physical body). Also, and importantly, you are not your social identity, although this too makes you what you are. Your "I" experience can be reduced neither to your reddish flesh body nor to your social consciousness or status (as in "title"). There is a true you that cannot be placed and located. It is just there. Observing but nowhere. Again, by accepting that the Self is nowhere and not seeing this as a puzzle to be explained away, one reaches a wisdom about oneself and reality that, arguably, explains more than conventional psychological theory. As Suzuki comments in *Zen Buddhism and Psychoanalysis*:

> Rinzai's "true man of no title" is no other than the one who is at this moment in front of every one of us, most assuredly listening to my voice as I talk or my word as I write. Is this not the most wonderful fact we all experience? Hence the philosopher's sense of "the mystery of being," if he has actually sensed it. We ordinarily talk of "I," but "I" is just a pronoun and is not the reality itself. I often feel like asking, "What does 'I' stand for? As long as 'I' is a pronoun like 'you' or 'he' or 'she' or 'it,' what is that which stands behind it? Can you pick it out and tell me, 'This is it'?" The psychologist informs us that "I" is nonexistent, that it is a mere concept designating a structure or an integration of relationships. But the strange fact is that when the "I" gets angry, it wants to destroy the whole world, together with the structure itself for which it is the symbol. Where does a mere concept derive its dynamics? What makes the "I" declare itself to be the only real thing in existence? The "I" cannot just be an allusion or a delusion, it must be something more real and substantial.[20]

Finally, the idea of our true non-self self being transcendent of cause and effect should too be seen as a declaration of truth rather than an irritating antinomy or contradiction. The old Kantian problem of whether humans are free or just one more part of nature should be seen not as a paradox but as the most profound description possible of the cosmos and our place in it. As Suzuki wrote in his *Studies in the Lankāvatāra Sutra*:

> According to the Mahāyāna, the outside world of form-and-name and the inner world of thought and feeling are both no more than the construction of mind, and when the mind ceases, the weaving-out of a world of particulars is stopped. This stopping is called emptiness or no-birth, but it is not the wiping out of existence, it is on the contrary viewing it truthfully unhampered by discriminative categories. Buddhism, therefore, upholds causation on the ground that things actually come into view and pass out of view, only it rejects the view that causation has its first term, has started from a primary cause or causal agent which is a fixed final reality.[21]

One key point about this view of the self and causality is that there is no escaping the world of phenomena. We are as we are in the absolute here and now. As should be clear by now, the true non-self self is not to be discovered on another mystical plane or in another realm transcendent of the material. You find the self as soon as you start looking for it because when you start looking you find there is no self and that it is this no self that is the self. It is paradoxical but your own very existence proves that it is true.

Zen and Psychoanalysis

Suzuki's importance as a Zen philosopher of the mind and the self perhaps lies most fully in his engagement with twentieth-century psychoanalysis, or rather its engagement with him. Similarly, Suzuki, as a Zen philosopher, was open to aligning Zen with the occult in its broadest manifestations. The three movements, *Zen*, *psychoanalysis*, and *the occult* not only present intriguing lines of overlap but also manifest crucial distinctions. In exploring these I wish to point out that Suzuki's fullest view of the self as no-self is ultimately a religious view based on a religious faith informed by a religious cosmology. As such, Zen's alliances with psychoanalysis and the occult can only ever be fleeting and partial. To explore this fully I will need to spend some time discussing the connections between psychoanalysis, the occult, and religion before presenting Suzuki's complete vision of the non-self, consciousness, and the greater cosmos.

Buddhism many thousands of years ago came up with ideas about the mind that the West only stumbled upon in any serious way at the end of the nineteenth century. Psychoanalysis, in particular, found itself sauntering into the same field that Buddhism has been furrowing since centuries past. Both psychoanalysis and Zen Buddhism, at the most general level, share the same model of the mind—there is a conscious self that is only one small part of an overall mind that includes subconscious and unconscious parts. And, crucially, those subconscious and unconscious parts are experienced as being something "other" to ourselves. *There is a part of our mind that acts as though it were someone else.* Both Zen and psychoanalysis recognize this "other" with the only controversy being how really much "other" to us it is.

Modern psychology arose inevitably with the evolutionary view of humans that emerged in the nineteenth century. William James in his ground-breaking *Psychology: Briefer Course* (1892) sought to discover the emergence of consciousness in biological nature. He wrote:

> The great fault of the older rational psychology was to set up the soul as an absolute spiritual being with certain faculties of its own by which the several activities of remembering, imagining, reasoning, willing, etc., were explained almost without reference to the peculiarities of the world with which these activities deal. But the richer insights of modern days perceives that our inner faculties are *adapted* in advance to the features of the world in which we dwell, adapted, I mean, so as to secure our safety and prosperity in its midst.[22]

He detected a certain primordial state of consciousness he dubbed "pure experience" a concept that was taken up by Nishida Kitaro to help him glue Zen and continental philosophy together.[23] But eventually modern psychology in the United States mostly deviated from James's pragmatic approach and went down instead the road of cognitive psychology where our minds are seen in purely materialist terms as events of neurology with the contents of our thoughts seen as secondary, if even seen as relevant at all. By contrast, psychoanalysis begins with content. It grasps our conscious thoughts and from there delves inward, downward, and deeper into the mind, dismissing those neurological aspects of conscious activity as mostly irrelevant.

Psychoanalysis and Religion

Psychoanalysis has always had a complicated relationship with religion. Freud and others tended to explain away religion as a symptom of the mind. We are religious and believe in God and the supernatural not because there is a God and the supernatural but because our human minds are designed to produce such beliefs. Our subconscious, that "other" in our head, vapors up into our conscious self notions of a big Other or big Others (in monotheism or polytheism versions) that we think are coming from the cosmos but are really coming from within our very own minds. Those *other* divine beings we think we see in nature or at the edge of our universe are really just projections from the *other* part of our own *self*. According to Eric Fromm, Freud saw the illusions of religion as something positive if properly clarified. The fact that your religious beliefs come from within yourself should enlighten you to the fact that your deepest desires are at one with your religious cravings making you as you are yourself a far more positive presence in the cosmos than your traditional religion may have led you to believe. On the other hand, and again I am following Fromm here, Carl Jung saw religion as ultimately delusional and a diversion from truth.[24] Either way, whether religion is a good thing or a bad thing, it was seen by the patriarchs of psychoanalysis as a state of mind, not actual true knowledge.

Psychoanalysis and the Occult

While psychoanalysis may have been dismissive of religion, it had a far more awkward relationship with the occult. It is hard to define the occult and differentiate it from religion, but let's go with Colin Wilson's working definition: "that there is a kind of 'psychic ether' that carries mental vibrations as the 'luminiferous ether' is supposed to carry light."[25] Freud, of course, as an arch-materialist would have nothing to do with occult claims and this was, on the surface, one of his reasons for falling out with Jung. But, even so, in a lecture titled "Dreams and Occultism" Freud recounts some strange cases that involve very strange coincidences which could amount to telepathy and the like.[26] Needless to say, he does not claim this outright but does point out, for example, how insects seem to communicate without language as though they did have language, and if such telepathic style behavior can be seen among insects where else in nature can it be seen? He leaves the question open. Jung was more explicitly welcoming of the claims of the occult. But according to Colin Wilson, he was very much conflicted over whether to pursue a respectable scientifically orthodox approach to his psychoanalysis or whether to embrace fully the paranormal claims of the occult.[27]

Why has psychoanalysis, that mostly respectable branch of science and psychology, been finding it so difficult to extricate itself from the obscurantist claims of the occult? It is because of the basic assumption that underlies psychoanalysis: our mind is bigger than our conscious self and, as individuals we carry within us both our own self-identity and this subconscious or unconscious other that is a stranger to us, while being a part of us. As Nishida Kitaro once famously wrote, "It is not that there is experience because there is an individual, but that there is an individual because there is experience."[28] One way of understanding the import of this is to set up a thought experiment (in both senses of the phrase). Imagine I can have full control of your mind, make you think certain things, to such an extent that even you do not know I am controlling you. In such a case are we still experiencing the world separately or are you now simply an appendage to my mind, one more bit of my experience of the world? Is experience the iCloud and you and I separate devices (as in "individuals")? Now, Nishida never, ever made these kinds of extrasensory claims but my point is that if we take on board Nishida's claim that (conscious) experience is more than the solitary self-contained self-identifying self-conscious individual, a claim psychoanalysis would also make, then it is easy to see how experience can, theoretically, escape the moorings of biological individuality and vibrate in the psychic ether. It is the stuff of science fiction rather than religious fantasy. For the "older rational psychology" with "the soul as an absolute spiritual being" (as James said), this was not a problem: there is experience because there is an individual. For the hardcore cognitive scientists too, it is not a problem. But for psychoanalysis, where individual self-conscious identity is not proof of an individual self, collapse into the "bad" science of the occult is always a danger.

How much or how little the psychoanalytic theorists can orbit clear of the occult depends on their idea of how "other" the other in our mind really is. Freud was a hardcore materialist whose model of the psyche was hermetic. His metaphors were hydraulic, closed systems of channels and pressures, allowing for no leaks into any "psychic ether." Jung's system was less well sealed. The "other" is possibly seeping in from the outside, perhaps due to our evolutionary inheritance. We are born with organs and bones the same as other animals. Perhaps the contents of our dreams, even at the most seemingly personal and individual level, are also products of nature, shared with other animals. This view of evolutionary biology, while heterodox, is still scientifically respectable. Or, the "other" could be seeping in because our thoughts can vibrate between one another in the ether, a far less scientifically approved claim. As Wilson maintains, Jung could not make up his mind up on this.

How Other Is Other?

And so, embarrassing and all as occult conclusions may be for psychoanalysis, the occult is still science, albeit "bad science," and not religion, in that the occult still claims natural and scientific explanations for its beliefs. An occultist can assert that psychic ether (let's say) is a part of nature as much as evolution and wave particles. In fact, occultism is arguably anti-religion in that in seeking scientific verification it is implying that religious faith is not the right vehicle for truth. Religion believes in the supernatural and a cosmology populated, and perhaps created, by divine beings. These are beliefs that, by definition, can only be grounded in faith, not scientific enquiry. Science can, theoretically, if we do not worry too much about correct methodology, make anything supernatural become natural and can turn any divine beings into physical energies. Science's job is to explain everything and that is precisely what it does. As the eminently occultist Charles Fort once wrote, "Science is a maw, or a headless and limbless stomach, an amoeba-like gut that maintains itself by incorporating the assimilable and rejecting the indigestible."[29]

If we were to ask what is the difference between the occult and religion it is, at core, that religion still holds an unscientific teleology, whereas the teleology of the occult conforms with the unintentional mechanical cosmology of science. This means that no matter what we find in nature that we find unusual, such as telepathic ants or teleporting quarks, it will not prove (nor disprove) the teleological claims of religion, but simply sit parallel to them. The claims of Zen, as espoused by Suzuki, could cohere with the scientific claims of psychoanalysis insofar as it disowns any religious-style claims to a cosmological teleology. Again, my argument will be that Zen does not do this and Suzuki always fell back into the religious aspects of Zen when pushed there by his interactions with psychoanalysis.

Suzuki and Occultism

Suzuki's Zen very much parallels the theoretical structures and stresses of psychoanalysis. The basic model of the mind, that of an individual consciousness embedded in a wider unconscious is Zen as much as it is psychoanalysis. From very early on in his 1896 work *Shinshukyoron* (『新宗教論』 *A New Interpretation of Religion*) Suzuki wished to make religion something that could sit easily with the scientific mind. With this, Suzuki constantly asserted the empirical nature of Zen, the fact that it is based on direct experience of one's own mind rather than a doctrine revealed to you by others. As with psychoanalysis, Suzuki also had a qualified openness to occultic thinking. He approved of the theosophy movement, which his wife was a part of. He also translated works by Emanuel Swedenborg and wrote books approving of the Swedish mystic and pointing out some of his affinities with Buddhist thought.[30]

In his work *Zen Buddhism and Psychoanalysis*, Suzuki explicitly links the unconscious of Zen to occult claims. He talks of a samurai who one day was able to sense the murderous fantasizing of an underling. From this, he comments more generally about the unusual sensory powers of trained samurai:

> This sensing of an unseen enemy seems to have developed among the swordsmen to a most remarkable degree of efficiency in those feudal days when the samurai had to be on the alert in every possible situation that might arise in his daily life. Even while in sleep he was ready to meet an untoward event. I do not know if this sense could be called a sixth sense or sort of telepathy and therefore a subject for parapsychology so-called.[31]

Here we see the usual slippage into occult thinking on the grounds that once we have exited our ordinary individual consciousness we have entered a bigger unconscious which may perhaps be beyond our own individuality, connected with the outer world in a way that orthodox science cannot yet, if ever, explain. As Suzuki further comments:

> … the fact is that the master swordsman possesses what we may designate the unconscious and that this state of mind is attained when he is no more conscious of his acts and leaves everything to something which is not of his relative consciousness. We call this something or somebody; because of its being outside the ordinary field of consciousness we have no word for it except to give it a negative name, X, or the unconscious.[32]

Now, his use of the term "X" to describe this unconscious connectivity beyond our consciousness is interesting because, through a curious, uncanny synchronicity (of course), it turns out that that is what Colin Wilson in his book *The Occult* calls it, "X," or rather "Faculty X, which is man's direct sense of reality."[33]

Suzuki's Zen was all about knowing the mind by exploring one's own mind. But the result would be that this exploration and the insights and awareness garnered from it would still the mind, cure our anxieties, and even offer salvation of an (almost) spiritual nature. It was both this theory and practice of Zen that made Zen an obvious fellow traveler with psychoanalysis and explains why two of the leading lights of twentieth-century psychoanalytical theory, Carl Jung and Eric Fromm were attracted to these parallels and sought to understand them further, with both of them reaching out to Suzuki.

Carl Jung and Suzuki

Carl Jung wrote a foreword for the 1939 German version of Suzuki's book *An Introduction to Zen Buddhism*. The introduction was later added to the English versions of the book and was highly influential in bringing Suzuki's work to the attention of a wider audience.[34] Jung, in a fairly orthodox mid-twentieth-century orientalist way, argued that Zen and satori (Zen awakening) was not accessible to Westerners, as it was too grand and mighty for those born into the rationalist and monotheist West. But satori can act as an inspiration to Westerners, "a beacon on a high mountain, shining out in the hazy future"[35] as to what can be achieved when we understand properly the construction of the self as understood by *both* Zen and psychoanalysis. Continuing his beacon on a high mountain metaphor, Jung comments:

> It would be an unhealthy mistake to assume that *satori* or *samadhi* are to be met with anywhere below these heights. For a complete experience there can be nothing cheaper or smaller than the whole. The psychological significance of this can be understood by the simple consideration of the fact that the conscious is only a part of the spiritual, and is never therefore capable of spiritual completeness: for that the indefinite expansion of the unconscious is needed.[36]

Although Jung tells us that he is not at all qualified to explain satori, he does actually go about explaining it in terms of the standard psychoanalytic model of the self. We have a consciousness which does not give us knowledge about the world but actually shuts off most of the world to us so that we can cope with the small sliver of knowledge consciously allowed to us. On the other hand, the unconscious is there, taking it all in, beaming its data to the consciousness which will filter out most of it. But satori is that moment when the conscious filter disappears and the unconscious, with all its data, with all its knowledge, with all its stimuli, with all its awareness of all that is before it, comes to the fore. With a bit of Zen training this does not lead to an overload or breakdown but to absolute awakening. Satori is hence utterly compatible with the psychoanalytic view of the unconscious. One further point is that Jung here is rejecting the notion that our unconscious is that which hides all our base animal instincts. Instead, the unconscious is something clean and wholesome, the source of all that is good in us. He says, "The unconscious is the matrix of all metaphysical assertions, of all mythology, all philosophy (in so far as it is not merely critical) and all forms of life which are based upon psychological suppositions."[37] This was one major source of tension between Jung and Freud: to what extent is the biological legacy of our consciousness something base or something noble. Evolution has produced both dogs and humans, who no doubt share the common trait of being conscious. In fact, there is so much consciously similar between dogs and humans that they very often end up becoming the very best of friends. There have been (semi-)scientific studies into the ability of dogs to understand the mind of their human friends and masters. One study suggests that dogs know when their human owner is planning to come home even when they are many miles apart.[38] But while they can display these remarkable occultic Faculty X abilities, dogs also engage in less spiritually advanced behaviors such as barking at birds and making love to sofas. When it comes to the animal unconscious, Jungian psychology would tend to emphasize canine telepathic tendencies whereas Freudians would be more interested in a dog's sofa humping instincts. Zen, in this account, is signed up to the Jungian project of delving into our clean unconsciousness to let it express its inner creative powers, in contrast to the Freudian project of tinkering with our dirty unconsciousness precisely with the intention of keeping it safely unconscious.

Erich Fromm and Suzuki

For Eric Fromm, the conflict between a clean and dirty unconscious was simply a misunderstanding. The unconscious is both.

> In Freud's thinking the unconscious is essentially that in us which is bad, the repressed, that which is incompatible with the demands of our culture and of our higher self. In Jung's system the unconscious becomes a source of revelation, a symbol for that which in religious language is God himself. In his view the fact that we are subject to the dictates of our unconscious is in itself a religious phenomenon. I believe that both these concepts of the unconscious are one-sided distortions of the truth. Our unconscious—that is, that part of our self which is excluded from the organized ego which we identity with our self—contains both the lowest and the highest, the worst and the best. We must approach the unconscious not as if it were a God whom we must worship or a dragon we must slay but in humility, with a profound sense of humor, in which we see that other part of ourselves as it is, neither with horror nor with awe.[39]

This dialectic between Jung and Freud in Fromm was very much characteristic of his style of thinking, something he shared with Suzuki who was also a great synthesizer (except for his bouts of occidentalist overstatement). Whenever there are two opposing points of view, we must assume that they are not actually opposing but are simply two sides of the one coin, or two wings on the same bird. This is how Suzuki too handled doctrinal differences between Rinzai and Soto Zen and between Zen and Pure Land Buddhism.[40]

Fromm was similarly engaged in a search for a third way between communism and capitalism, and discovered it in a philosophy of what could be described as "individualism," the idea that liberation is to be sought and found within one's own consciousness. This was, of course, a view of things Zen would be very familiar with, the dream of detachment from repressive social structures and the discovery of one's truly free and real (non-)selfhood behind the socially constructed one. The added hope from Fromm was that this act of inner liberation would feed back into society, creating a wider liberated consciousness at a group level. This is in many ways the ideals of the "1960s" encapsulated. Individual freedom at the level of inner consciousness to shape a better society for all. It was mass socialism and Nietzschean elitism combined, and Zen was to be a weapon in the campaign. It is easy to be cynical about this, write it off as bourgeois Zen, and dismiss it as self-help therapy for the middle classes who want to liberate their minds but not much else. But the "consciousness" of the 1960s, with its emphasis on human rights and equality, its assertion of how truly we are all people of "no title" (as Rinzai would say), is something that still resonates and something from which we continue to benefit. Indeed, (to digress) individualism and respect for inner consciousness is still, one could argue, winning the cold war in a nicer way for us by clearing a middle path between glacial communist-style group think and icy hearted neoliberal capitalism.[41]

Although Eric Fromm and Carl Jung were born from the same psychoanalytic stable and certainly shared the same liberationist views of psychotherapy, there was a difference between them. Jung was a romantic traditionalist who saw us as inheriting a content-specific consciousnesses from our culture which we tended to be stuck with, and which was why Jung did not see the possibility of Zen being transferable to the West. Fromm, on the other hand, saw our consciousness as something far more flexible, empty, and free. We are not stuck with our culture nor are we stuck in the past. We are only stuck when our individual minds are possessed by those economic systems that alienate the individual.

> It is not that Western Man cannot fully understand Eastern systems, such as Zen Buddhism (as Jung thought), but that modern Man cannot understand the spirit of a society that is not centered in property and greed.[42]

Zen is not something on a distant mountain to gaze at, as Jung seemed to argue, but something that can be carried down into the lives of Westerners to be understood and practiced with varying degrees of intensity, depending, of course and as always, on the individual. It was with this spirit of openness that Fromm arranged a conference on Zen and psychoanalysis in Mexico in 1957, with D. T. Suzuki as the central speaker and lecturer.

Flower Power

The conference resulted in the book titled, unsurprisingly, *Zen and Psychoanalysis*, containing Suzuki's talks at the conference, along with contributions from Fromm and Richard DeMartino. Suzuki's text is a remarkable work and displays every bit of what was both wonderful and infuriating about his talks and writings. Long, long quotes, with the occasional odd jump between sometimes random points, but a powerful vision, pumped and pumped, of a different consciousness that leaves the reader stunned through its gripping glimpses of things very different and profound. What is very obvious from the beginning of the text is that Suzuki is, by nature, more a Jungian than a Frommian. In the first section he makes a clear distinction between eastern and western ways of thinking, which he summarizes through a comparison of two poems by Tennyson and the haiku poet Basho. Both poets see a flower, but Tennyson picks (and kills) the flower and ponders upon it, whereas Basho just reacts momentarily and moves on. The rational, analytic, and aggressive West versus the intuitive, synthetic, and passive east. (Fromm, the indefatigable dialectician, in a later work adds a third poem by Goethe to overcome this duality. Goethe sees a flower, ponders it, but transplants it so that it can flourish better.) There is a clear divide between Suzuki's orientalist Zen elitism, which Jung admired and asserted, and the New Age popular cosmopolitanism that Fromm came to represent. But Suzuki's message of Zen was always bigger than his own old-fashioned tendencies, and after this Orientalist opening, his talk proceeds to explain where Zen consciousness is to be found in psychoanalysis. The answer is at the very, very bottom of our consciousness, which is also its very, very surface. And as such, Zen is not really to be found in psychoanalysis, but rather psychoanalysis is to be found in Zen. This is clear when he starts going down through all the different layers of consciousness and unconsciousness that are to be broken through when a koan (Zen riddle) is to be solved:

> The head is conscious while the abdomen is unconscious. When the master tells his disciples to 'think' with the lower part of the body, he means that the koan is to be taken down to the unconscious and not to the conscious field of consciousness. The koan is to 'sink' into the whole being and not stop at the periphery. Literally, this makes no sense, which goes without saying. But when we realize that the bottom of the unconscious where the koan 'sinks' is where even the ālaya-vijñāna, "the all-conserving consciousness" cannot hold it, we see that the koan is no more in the field of intellection, it is thoroughly identified with one's Self. The koan is now beyond all the limits of psychology.
>
> When all these limits are transcended—which means going even beyond the so-called collective unconscious—one comes upon what is known in Buddhism as ādarśañājñana, 'mirror knowledge.' The darkness of the unconscious is broken through and one sees all things as one sees one's face in the brightly shining mirror.[43]

A diagram describing these layers would not be hard to draw. We can picture a pyramid with an arrow going down. We start with the conscious at the top and go down into the unconscious, then through the (Jungian) collective unconscious, which Suzuki (probably unintentionally) places beyond the limits of psychology. The next level is the ālaya-vijñāna, which is definitely beyond consciousness, this then is broken through and the arrow zooms back up again to the conscious with the label "ādarśañājnana" added to the arrow. This all makes sense because, when we think about it, while the conscious includes the unconscious, the unconscious must also include the conscious, perhaps even more so. It is impossible for the unconscious to "think" without the conscious. Suzuki's model is admirably inclusive and integrative of all these layers, especially with the curious swing of the ādarśañājnana back to the top. Suzuki, a few pages later, further explains this ādarśañājnana. And here he adds two very important concept (prajñā and karuṇā) which will totally shake and then shift his entire psychoanalytical edifice into a religious zone.

The ādarśañājnana which reveals itself when the bottom of the unconscious, that is, of the ālaya-vijñāna, is broken through, is no other than prajñā-intuition. The primary will out of which all beings come is not blind and unconscious; it seems so because of our ignorance (avidyā) which obscures the mirror, making us oblivious even of the fact of its existence. The blindness is on our side and not on the side of the will, which is primarily and fundamentally noetic as much as conative. The will is prajñā plus karuṇā, wisdom plus love. On the relative, limited, finite plane, the will is seen as revealed fragmentally; that is to say, we are apt to take it as something separated from our mind-activities. But when it reveals itself in the mirror of ādarśañājnana, it is "God as he is." In him prajñā is not differentiated from karuṇā.

Prajñā and Karuṇā

The problem is that in using these two terms, Suzuki has shunted Zen from being something that is empirical and compatible with science (even if it veers into the quasi-occultic) to something religious, that is based on belief and faith rather than experience. By evoking prajñā, Suzuki is saying that the cosmos has an intentionality ("The primary will out of which all beings come is not blind and unconscious") which means, in effect, it has a personhood, another consciousness if you like, that knows you are here. Not only that, but this other personhood likes that you are here, in fact, It (or He or She) likes everything that is here. It (or He or She) feels karuṇā, or love. What is this personhood? It cannot be part of one's own self as that would be pantheistic or even solipsistic. It must entail an other, a big Other if you like. This big Other has a will which is separate to us. Note carefully Suzuki's language on this: "the blindness is on our side and not on the side of the will." There is us here and this "will" over there on the other side. Now, Suzuki may argue that when we *experience* enlightenment we *know* the will is prajñā plus karuṇā, and hence the scientific claims of Zen are sustained. But how do we "know" it is prajñā plus karuṇā, and that we are not delusional about this. We do not know the "I" experience of another, all we do assume is that it is there for them. Unless I actually become you absolutely I cannot know you absolutely. Science can never penetrate this far where you are capable of experiencing the will of another as yourself, even the will of the cosmos. To assert that the will, as in "the primary will out of which all beings come," is wisdom and love is a religious claim no matter how much we may seek to couch it in psychological terms.

In linking Zen to prajñā and karuṇā as he does, Suzuki is also giving Zen a teleology, which is the final shove for Zen into the realm of religion. The Zen vision is not of a mechanical cosmos where things whirl and turn for no reason and forces move with no mind of their own. Instead it is a vision of a cosmos that is governed by a wisdom and love which we can discover and experience through our own penetration of our own minds. As with, as we shall see, Sudhana in the Gaṇḍavyūha Sutra, we start on our journey to find wisdom and eventually find it because it comes seeking us. This is the story of our lives, the purpose of the cosmos, the teleology of humanity. The love and wisdom of the primary will is our salvation and the meaning of why we are here.

The Big Other is not the Big Other

But this primary will imbued with prajñā and karuṇā is not to be seen as a separate God, a separate being standing against us as a big Other. If we do take this primary will to be distinct from us we are suffering from delusion, or avidyā. We are like those who confuse the voices from their own unconscious to be the voices of another. This confusion is very obvious in pathological cases of hallucination. But Zen Buddhism would argue that it is a problem we all share, albeit less acutely. We all suffer from avidyā. We are all ensnared by an inner sense of a great Other that is watching over the cosmos that He/She/It created. We think He/She/It is out there when in fact it is our own minds that create it. There is no great Other, only our greater Self.

Lacanian psychoanalysis, which carries on the Freudian dirty consciousness tradition, too believes that there is no big Other.[44] This coalescence between Lacanian and Zen Buddhist philosophies has piqued the interest of Slavoj Žižek and in his book *Less than Nothing* he engages in an extensive discussion on the contrasts between Lacanianism and what he dubs "Western Buddhism."[45] Žižek sees a division between Lacanianism and Buddhism in terms of two related questions: how did we get into this delusion situation, this *samsara*, where we believe in a big Other that is not there, and how do we get out of this same delusional situation. How did we get in? How do we get out? For a materialist Lacanian, how we get in is presumably a product of biology and evolution which has granted us our self-deluding psyches. How we get out is by killing our own religious projections deriving from this deluded notion of a big Other and replacing it with a belief in a social big Other, which is delusional but not so much that we cannot recognize it to be our own creation. Žižek seems to be recognizing that we cannot ever get rid of the big Other in our minds—a recognition that scientism, which believes in the fantasy that religion can be overcome simply through rational thinking, lacks.[46]

How does Buddhism answer the question: how did we get in? Looking at Suzuki, there seem to be many answers that are all unclear and awkward. In the *Zen and Psychoanalysis* talk, his answer seems to be that we cannot know why we are delusional when we are delusional. He quotes Paul (I Corinthians 13: 12): "At present, we are looking at a confused reflection in a mirror; then, we shall see face to face; now, I have only glimpses of knowledge; then I shall recognize God as he has recognized me." He glyphs this with the explanation that "'at present' or 'now' refers to relative and finite time-sequence, while 'then' is eternity, which, in my terminology, is prajñā-intuition. In prajñā-intuition or 'knowledge' I see God as he is in himself."[47] You won't know how you got in until you get out. Elsewhere, Suzuki seems to answer it, metaphorically, in a Fall of Man style explanation. Humans, like all other animals, were not in the delusions of samsara to begin with until they did something that messed with their own psyches. For example, he states "human consciousness was so made that at the beginning there was utter not-knowing. Then there was the eating of the fruit of the tree of knowledge—the knowledge that consists in making the knower different from what he knows. That is the origin of this world."[48] Elsewhere, he blames God. "When God created the world outside Himself, He made a great mistake. He could not solve the problem of the world as long as He kept it outside of Himself."[49]

One thing we must note is that Suzuki never explains it through random biological evolution. Our minds did not just arise in nature because DNA that gives rise to minds does better in the competition for survival. There is something about the human mind that is more than just the mechanics of the brain. From whither comes the human mind? It comes from the big Other, that intentional wise and loving consciousness which we must know and recognize through knowing and recognizing our own selves. This is why the question of how we got in is so difficult for Suzuki because it concludes in a faith-based cognizance of the personhood of the big Other. The scientific answer, even in occult science, to the question of how we got in here will never recognize a non-materialist, non-biological big Other. Suzuki's original project, as expressed in his early book *Shinshukyoron* (1896) to make religion empirical and compatible with science will always reach an impasse at this point.

Where Žižek would say that there is no big Other but we have to experience the world as though there is, Suzuki will say, there is a big Other but we have to experience the world as though there is not. This denial is the only way that Suzuki can combine the concept of karuṇā (the love of the primary will) with the notion of a non-self. It is, effectively, to engage in a religious leap of faith—the big Other to be found within our greater self as non-self is all-wise (prajñā) and all loving (karuṇā). The will that gave rise to the cosmos, that got us in here, is a loving will which aims to get us out of here. It is a will that knows us and loves us as though we were other to it when in fact we are not. There is nothing at all wrong with this belief so long as one recognizes that it is a belief, a religious belief, and not something you just know naturally through empirical enquiries into your own consciousness.

As we shall see in the next chapter, how much Zen knowledge is empirical and how much is faith is a thorny issue in the philosophy of Zen.

Knowledge

Zen knowledge

As we have seen in our discussion of the self in Zen, it is important to understand that the distinction between the subject (you) and the object (the world you are looking at) is ultimately false. In a similar way, the distinction between a knower and what is known is also misguided. The truest knowledge we have, knowledge that we can absolutely affirm is knowledge that exists without a knower and that which is known. It is knowledge that is simply knowledge with no dualities of subject/object, knower/known dividing it.

Two in One

To understand dualism and its problems, it is useful to think about monism. And so let us ask, what is monism? It is the idea that all is one. The argument for this can be made with the very simple assertion that two things can always be united into one larger object (or concept) that will encompass both. If I have two objects, let's say two pencils, I can place them into a pencil holder to make them part of one larger object. We could continue this process for the whole universe. Every material bit of it can be categorized into something larger. Until we reach God who can also be placed along with His universe into a wider concept— call it the One, or the All, or whatever. Paul Carus, the German-American philosopher for whom Suzuki worked and collaborated as a young man, was famously monistic, making the argument that the universe and God were one, with the latter evolving in the form of the former. For him, monism was simply the common-sense view that everything must be consistently every thing. He wrote: "Monism stands upon the principle that all the different truths are but so many different aspects of one and the same truth. Two truths may be complementary to each other, but there cannot be two truths contradictory to each other. There is but one truth, and that one truth is eternal. Monism, in a word, signifies consistency."[1] But the problem is that Carus's monism is an exclusively naturalist and objectivist one. It is built from a materialist observation of the world of objects as they are and extends this to the rest of the cosmos from there, finishing with one all-inclusive concept to round off the monist vision. This is a very different vision, let's say, to the cosmology presented by the Buddhist sutra the Gaṇḍavyūha. Here we see a mind-bending world where space and time are warped at will by celestial beings, and where each bit of the world contains within itself a myriad of other worlds. There is no consistent time or spatial extension, just eternal juxtaposings as objects defy each other's dimensions. The Gaṇḍavyūha Sutra is the story of Sudhana, a young pilgrim searching for wisdom. He comes across a tower known as the Vairochana Tower. Suzuki describes what he sees upon entering it.

> And within this Tower, spacious and exquisitely ornamented, there are hundreds of thousands of asamkhyeyas ["Literally, innumerable" (Suzuki's footnote)] of towers, each one of which is as exquisitely ornamented as the main Tower itself and as spacious as the sky … Sudhana the young pilgrim sees himself in all the towers as well as in each single tower, where all is contained in one and each contains all.[2]

The monism described herein is not about stretching out from here to infinity, but all of infinity stretching itself into here.

Spot the Difference

Material monism is, in some respects, just a matter of terminology. There will always be a word for everything to create a concept of all.

A deeper monist defying crack opens up in the cosmos when we consider not the objects out there but you that is looking at them. Here Oneness is less unitary. To understand this let us use a simple thought experiment. Imagine one of those "spot the difference" puzzle pictures you have no doubt seen many times in comics or magazines. On the left there is a picture of a desk with a pencil holder containing two pencils in it. On the right, is a picture with just the desk with no holder or anything else on it. How many differences are there between the picture on the left and the picture on the right? One? (No filled pencil holder in the right-hand picture.) Or three? (No pencil holder or two pencils in the picture on the right.) In other words, is the pencil holder filled with two pencils one object or three? You may have your answer but pay attention to how what constitutes an object can change, not due to chemistry or physics, but due to our perceptions. Two pencils lying beside a pencil holder would constitute three different objects, but put the pencils into the holder and for many people we would now have just one object. Here we see the real duality in the world, between the Subject (the viewer looking at the world) and the Object (as in all the objects out there in the world being looked at).

The subject-object relationship is from where knowledge arises. A subject looks at an object and knows it. But which is determining this knowledge, the subject or the object? We could argue, for example, that it is the subject. Whether a pencil holder with two pencils in it is one object or three is decided by the subject. If the subject looks away any distinctions between the objects are not seen by the subject and hence are not there. An example of such a subject-oriented approached to knowledge would be George Berkeley at his wildest. Another answer is to say that all knowledge lies with the object. The objects of the world are there unchanging. The pencils do not change size or atomic structure just because they are placed in a holder. The world does not change just because opinions about the varieties of its objects in it change. This view is the materialist, perhaps scientism view. There is a third view and that is to argue that both subject and object are involved in the constitution of knowledge. Both of them are contributing to the act of knowing.

Perhaps the subject gives the sense of space and time for the object to exist in, and the object gives the concept of itself, as in "pencilness," for the subject to recognize it. This is very broadly the Kantian view. And so we have three possible scenarios: knowledge comes from the subject; knowledge comes from the object; knowledge comes from both subject and object. Can there be a fourth answer? There can and it is the one Suzuki promoted—knowledge comes when there is no subject and no object.

We may grumble that this is madness since we experience the world through a subject-object dichotomy. But do we? How often do you know an object as an object? You may grab a pencil to write down a memo, but you would have great difficulty remembering what color the pencil was, if you ever actually "knew" it at all. We go through the world not knowing each object, just maneuvering with the minimum of conscious recognition of our surroundings. You know something only when you need to or when something has gone wrong, something has hindered your progress through the world. But this is relative knowledge, or "vijnana." As Suzuki defines it: "Vijnana is our relative knowledge in which subject and object are distinguishable, including both knowledge of concrete particular things and that of the abstract and universal."[3] Our conscious knowledge is Vijnana, ranging from random thoughts about what groceries we must buy today to careful deliberations on legal affairs, from simple ideas about where to place your television remote control to complex analysis of microbiological processes. Such knowledge involves consciously looking at the world, consciously discerning objects in it, and consciously making judgments about those objects. But this knowledge, important and essential to life as it is, remains always partial and incomplete. It deals with reality over there and then, it can never, ever get at the reality here and now. This knowledge of here and now is a different kind of knowledge, which could be termed prajñā, or "unconscious consciousness." As Suzuki explains:

> However much of Vijnana we may accumulate, we can never find our abode of rest in it, for we somehow feel something missing in the

inmost part of our being, which science and philosophy can never appease. Science and philosophy do not apparently exhaust Reality; Reality contains more things than that which is taken up by our relative knowledge for our investigation. What is still left in Reality, according to Buddhism, turns towards Prajna for its recognition. Prajna corresponds to "unconscious consciousness" ...[4]

The point is that conscious knowing is derivative. It is secondary to a purer consciousness going on in the background as you go on your way. One way of thinking about this is to consider, however crudely, the difference between "knowing" and "seeing." Knowing involves making distinctions, violently bracketing off one part of reality from the rest. Seeing, on the one hand, is a non-judgmental embracement of all before you. Furthermore, knowing involves a knower, someone to make the judgments that constitute the knowledge. On the other hand, the act of seeing just happens. It is as though body and mind have dropped away,[5] as they say in Zen, and all that is there is there.

Zen descriptions of seeing and acting are rigorous in their rejection of the thinking mind. The better state to be in is no-mind (*mushin* 無心). We see this constantly in Suzuki's descriptions of Zen arts where automaticity in behavior is celebrated. The archer does not shoot the arrow. The arrow is shot without the archer consciously thinking about it. But a possible criticism here is to question whether unconscious seeing is superior to conscious knowing. It is merely a simpler state of mind that animals probably share with us. The archer firing his arrow in a state of *mushin* is no different to an amoeba eating plankton. But let us take the regression further, let us make another move beyond the seeing, and argue that behind this seeing is actual knowledge. It is knowledge of the form that does not include a subject-object division.

When subject and object do disappear, when body and mind drop away, when seer and seen are one, you do not get unicellular automatons, but a knowledge endowed with absolute certainty. To visualize this let us go back to those towers within towers as seen in the Gaṇḍavyūha

Sutra. The image is a stark rejection of the idea that time and space are something consistently extended and that objects are discretely presented to us. Instead, everything can fold into everything and all is interpenetrated. As Suzuki comments:

> The fundamental insight of the Gandavyuha is known as Interpenetration. It is, philosophically speaking a thought somewhat similar to the Hegelian conception of concrete-universals. Each individual reality, besides being itself, reflects in it something of the universal, and at the same time it is itself because of other individuals. A system of perfect relationship exists among individual existences and also between individuals and universals, between particular objects and general ideas.[6]

The other important message this cosmological picture gives us is that any one point is the center of all the rest. There is no God-like viewpoint, no all-embracing observer looking down on the whole. Instead, the all is to be seen at any one point. It is worth pondering the structure of knowledge being presented here. Everything is seen from one point, but that one point does not itself stand back from the all. This is the knowledge behind seeing: that you are there at one point at which all infinity is gathered. It is impossible to be aware of this with a rational mind. In fact, the role of the rational mind is to filter this vision, to let us see the world coherently but partially that we may manipulate it with a calculating mind. When the filter is lifted infinity is seen and known.

Zen makes the same point as the Gaṇḍavyūha, that reality is not what you know but what you really see if you could look properly at it. But this does not depend on a mind-blown imagination. To know infinity within infinity (those towers within towers) one just has to be aware of the here and now, and know that *here* is spatially infinite and *now* is temporally eternal. Of course, as we start getting into descriptions of this knowledge, rational explanation starts to break down. Already when we make mention of the eternal *now* and the infinite *here* the lights start flickering, the fuses start blowing, and the wires start smoking, as the ship of reason reaches the outer limits of rational knowledge to plunge into the blackhole of formless self-awareness from which only the random blips of the Zen koan, those Zen riddles, can be heard.

Satori

The goal of Zen, Suzuki tells us, is *satori*. This is knowledge, but not as we know it. It is the knowledge that emerges, or explodes, when the duality of subject and object is fully conquered and all that remains is just knowing. Attaining full *satori* is a rare achievement beyond most of us. It is something that can simply be attested to by accounts of Zen monks and practitioners over the ages. However, *satori* is also knowledge at its purest and simplest as it involves no external learning. With satori there is nothing you have to learn about. The learning just happens, all at once, in full form. You know it inside personally and no external authority can deny this knowledge since only you know it. Suzuki states:

> Satori is thus a form of perception, an inner perception, which takes place in the most interior part of consciousness. Hence the sense of authoritativeness, which means finality. So, it is generally said that Zen is like drinking water, for it is by one's self that one knows whether it is warm or cold. The Zen of perception being the last term of experience, it cannot be denied by outsiders who have no such experience.[7]

Although satori is "authoritative and final,"[8] Suzuki also points out that "there is a gradation in satori as to its intensity, as in all our mental activity."[9] Satori is a personal experience that only you can know you have had. Satori, also, does not have to be the full-blown mind-blown version of Tang period Zen lore. Let us then take Suzuki at his word here: *nobody can ever tell you that you have not satori-ed*. This is important because I want to emphasize here that most of us, maybe all of us, (it is impossible to check, of course) have some direct idea of what satori is about because most of us, maybe all of us, have experience gradations of it. Anyone with a conscious human mind will have glimpsed it at some moment in their life. Unfortunately, Suzuki at times in his writings tended to talk up the mysteries of satori and be dismissive of the unwashed laity's attempts to comprehend it, especially in the case of those who did not share Suzuki's nationality. For instance, although all praising of Eugene Herrigel's book *Zen in the Art of Archery* when he wrote a preface for it, Suzuki also remarked years later in 1959: "Herrigel is trying to get to Zen, but he hasn't grasped Zen itself. Have you ever seen a book written by a Westerner that has?"[10] The condescension in this remark is irritating to say the least. But for me, Suzuki was at his ugliest the day he made the following remarks in an interview in Japan about fellow Zen philosopher Alan Watts: "Oh, that guy Watts is a fake."[11] Alan Watts was a lifetime admirer of Suzuki and always believed that the two were on friendly terms.[12] So this comment indeed is a cruel betrayal. It is hard to know why Suzuki lashed out like this, playing the hardman in front of a home crowd. Watts himself wrote books about Zen which were similar in content to Suzuki's and made roughly the same arguments.[13] Suzuki didn't like that Watts had not formally practiced much zazen, but Suzuki's own formal practice and institutional status was always itself a bit vague.[14] Watts and Suzuki were more similar than they were different. It seems that, sadly, we must conclude that Suzuki was demonstrating yet again that absolute satori wisdom does not make one absolutely wise in every way, as in his strange unwisely chauvinist and unbuddhist assumption that only Asians can do satori properly. And so, in willful and intentional and open defiance of Suzuki's petty prejudices, I will talk and explain here what satori is about. It is not hard because, as I have said, probably all of us have experienced inklings of it. I remember as a teenager one day having a casual chat with a friend, we'll call him Liam (not his real name), about the meaning of life and religion and such things. Liam described to me how during one class in school the previous week he had, for a few moments, suddenly found himself staring at the teacher's nose and feeling overwhelmed by a sense of awe, "why are there noses"? He found himself utterly unable to tune himself back into regular reality for those moments. It seems a simple question but it is every bit as profound as Spinoza's why is there all this instead of nothing? Liam was in the throes of "knowledge" of a different experience. Our existence here now is a mystery. But most of the time we do not see it to be such. It is actually very hard to induce the sense of mystery we really should feel about our being in the world. Instead, our mind shoves the question to one side and fills itself up with the stuff of everyday mundanity. And this is how it should be. We would go mad if we really knew how mad our being here is. But sometimes the healthy filter we have to keep away the overwhelming awe we would have if we were *really* in our right minds suddenly melts and the mystery gushes in. For my friend Liam, for me on a few other occasions, and probably for you, it amounts to an instant. For enlightened Zen practitioners, by Suzuki's account, the sudden knowledge seems more certain and permanent.

The point about this awe and sudden rupture in everyday commonsense thinking that is both the launching pad and trajectory of satori is that it concerns not knowledge about the world but knowledge about the here and now. Zen is full of discussion about "here" and "now" and this is what we must be thinking about when we ponder the meaning and experience of satori. Questions about the world are answerable with information in the world and occasionally our information about the world may feel awe inspiring. For instance, "According to astronomer Dr Peter Edwards, if our solar system was a grain of sand, then The Milky Way (our Galaxy) would be 1,000 times the size of Durham Cathedral."[15] Now that is absolutely mind-blowing. But with a bit of reflection we can see that it is not the same as the awe we can feel about the here and now. Information about the world simply refits itself to suit our perceptions. The size of our Galaxy may be amazing but once we know it we can file away that knowledge with everything else we know. Indeed, the second time we hear such facts we do not feel so overwhelmed. On the other hand, awe about your existence in the here and now is deeply personal and devoid of any information by which you can readjust your mind to it. It is a mystery that finishes where it starts, you and your awareness of here and now. It can go no further because there is nowhere further to go.[16]

External information, such as star distances, is information that is out there in the world. The rupture, the break, the great doubt, the disturbance experienced in the here and now, about the here and now, has to be answered in the here and now. This means that scientific theories and information (such as biological evolution or cognitive science) cannot ever, by their very own nature, solve it. But this is also the problem with religious knowledge, it too is coming from out there in the world. This includes God and even the historical Buddha. These are external objects of knowledge and do not apply to knowledge of the here and now which, when fully realized, is satori. More than that, the fact that the answer is here and now means that language itself in every way breaks down since language, the ultimate instrument of dualist thinking, depends on those parts of space beyond here and those instances of time beyond now to be able to state anything meaningful. When it is about here and now there is nothing that can be possibly said.

Koans

But things are said and this is where we come to the famous koans of Zen. Koans are apparently non-sensical bits of dialog that ancient, usually Tang Dynasty Chinese Zen, masters engaged in. Examples of this abound in Suzuki. Here a two:

> A monk asked Tung-shan, "Who is the Buddha?" "Three chin of flax."[17]

> A monk asked Chao-chou, "What is the meaning of the First Patriarch's visit to China?' 'The cypress tree in the front courtyard."[18]

In fact, examples of koans in Suzuki's books often overtook the text, sometimes even distracting from and obscuring the wider points he was trying to make. Zen historian John R. McRae comments,

> … one can hardly read a page of twentieth-century writings on Zen without encountering the use of story as explanatory device. The most notable practitioner of this strategy is of course D. T. Suzuki, whose

standard approach is effectively to write that 'Zen is such-and-such, and let me tell a few stories that exemplify what I mean,' with little or no real attempt at explanation.[19]

As McRae's acidic comment suggests, Suzuki's use of koans are not without controversy. Firstly, koans were written down many centuries after the alleged dialog had taken place. It would be naïve to think these spontaneous outbursts were not, post facto, scripted. Also, Suzuki, like many other Zen scholars in his day, often did not understand fully the specific Chinese dialect they were written in. Furthermore, Suzuki's assumption that koans were arational and absurd meant that he often failed to see the inner logic and generic norms of the koan tradition.[20] To think about this, let us look at an example of a koan from our own day. In February 2000, when Linda Cutts was being installed as the new Abbot of the San Francisco Zen Center, one of her parishioners, Darlene Cohen, during the ceremony, decided to engage her in a spontaneous koan dialog, with Linda invited to go first. Michael Downing takes up the story: "'Knock, knock,' says Linda, sort of laughing already. Darlene looks really happy and pretty interested when she says, 'Who's there?'" "'It's Darlene,' says Linda."[21] The exchange is absurd. And yet, for those of us familiar with the genre of knock-knock jokes, it is actually very clever and witty. Not only that, but from the perspective of non-dual non-selfhood it does kind of make sense. But just imagine the challenges people will have trying to explain this koan in a 1,000 years' time.

However, even if it be the case that Suzuki talked up the spontaneity and absurdity of koans more than he should have, and even if he was using them in a secular context away from their proper institutional usage within Zen temples, the fact remains that the Zen tradition did produce voluminous examples of koans and mondos that are unusual for their seeming lack of coherence. Any mistranslations or interpretations of koans by Suzuki do not undermine his central point that koans in Zen were a product of Zen's special approach to the philosophy of language. Suzuki sometimes described koans as inevitable and unthought reactions to the experience of satori, like unintended groans of joy from one who has had their thirst for the ultimate knowledge satiated.[22] Other times, koans function as a form of communication between the initiated when initially initiating.[23] But whether they be sighs of soteriological satisfaction or signals of satori standardization, koan craziness asserts a deep message about the nature of language and knowledge.

Satori, we will remember, is knowledge of here and now in the here and now. Such knowledge can never be represented or expressed since this would involve the use of that which is not of the here and now. When our consciousness is not of the here and now it is looking out onto the world, dividing the world into its different objects, making judgments, consciously or not, of how the objects of the world are to be classified, used, and maneuvered. This, as we have pointed out, is how dualistic subject-object knowledge works: the subject looking at the world and knowing what is there in it. This knowledge can be expressed through signs, by attaching signs to the objects of knowledge. There is even the epistemologically delightful fact that signs themselves can become objects to be represented by other signs.[24] On and on it can go, ad infinitum, knowledge creating itself through ever splitting signs that will never reach a totality that can be finally known. Again, it is this non-stop generation of knowledge through the subject-object distinction, that makes philosophical and scientific knowledge inferior to the total knowledge of satori to be offered by Zen. It also reveals why words are useless when we are dealing with the knowledge that arises when there is no subject or object. With no subject or object there is nothing to attach our words and signs to, and no one to read those signs and know what they mean. To put it another way, words deal with space and time, carving them up into objects and events to be labelled and interpreted by a knowing subject. When we are dealing with the here and now, where there is no extension of space (it is absolutely here, not there), and no dimension of time (it is absolutely now, not a moment sooner or later) words simply fail. They cannot operate. They are useless. Not only useless but a barrier and distraction to knowledge of and from the here and now. Zen, that absolute knowledge of the here and now, simply cannot be explained, expressed, or communicated in words.

What Use Satori?

Satori is, by Suzuki's account, total knowledge since it is based on the dissolution of the subject-object distinction in the here and now. This gives it a complete self-evident obviousness. You never doubt, whatever else, that you are here, now. You just are. The fact of it is just there. Knowing this doesn't even depend upon you thinking about it. That is how certain and total satori knowledge is. It is apodictic, absolutely. Satori knowledge is also non-rational. Rationality is essentially about finding a coherent and patterned description of events and truths in the world out there. In this sense, rationality is dependent on a dualist vision. Satori applies to here and now. It cannot provide any data for rational judgments about its own event. It is just known without any reasoning. There is no description of it possible beyond the mere statement that it has occurred. It is not hard to see how the Buddhist concept of sunyata (空 emptiness) or mu (無 nothingness) can be easily linked to satori. The place where satori happens is no place. The time when it happens is no time. The knowledge that is acquired is no knowledge. This is not about negation. It is about that which is there prior to the differentiations of being. Neither is it about all beings being stuck together to form a great One (in the crudest monist sense) nor is it about subtracting being to get a purer and less messy state of being, a sparser minimal world with less noise and less bytes. It is not that I take away being to get nothingness but that I take away nothingness to get being. I empty emptiness to world my world. The eternal infinite here and now known through satori can only be an absolute emptiness. Anything more than that would be less than that.

However, absolute total and non-rational knowledge does have its problems, philosophically. The first problem is the one summarized in a withering comment by the Japanese philosopher Fukuzawa Yukichi (福沢諭吉 1835–1901): "Even if you let [Zen Patriarch] Bodhidharma sit in front of a wall for ninety years, he would never be able to invent the steam engine or the telegraph."[25] In other words, what is the use in knowing useless knowledge. Suzuki's answer would be that knowledge of satori and the knowledge needed to invent a lightbulb are not incompatible and should not be placed together in opposition. While Suzuki does see scientific knowledge as something inferior to the knowledge of satori, he does not see it as wrong or to be avoided.[26] On the contrary, Suzuki is forever at pains to point out that satori does not lead to withdrawal from society. He very often quoted the old Zen master, Baizhang Huaihai's [Japanese: Hyakujō Ekai] (720–814) dictum that a day without working is a day without eating.[27] There is nothing *impractical* about the absolute knowledge gained from self-awakening. Nor, for that matter, is there anything *practical* about it either. Satori does not at all endow the awakened with superhero abilities. It does not grant you special Jedi-like powers or a mystical third eye. As Suzuki comments, "The Buddhists do not practice self-concentration in order to acquire any miraculous power such as hearing heavenly sounds or seeing heavenly sights."[28]

Libertines

It is a fact that Zen's liberation cries, irrational sloganeering, calls for consciousness transformations, and the wild antics of its masters in distant times, attracted a diverse audience often extending to misfits and non-conformists who saw the koan-spouting self-transcending Tang monks as fellow comrades in the revolt against bourgeois morality.[29] These Beatnik social rebels with their degenerate lifestyles were not to Suzuki's taste. While, of course, Suzuki was entitled to his views and standards of social etiquette, we must recognize that philosophically there was a problem here. Suzuki had preached a Zen devoid of any outside authority since it involves knowledge that is completely personal and individual. As R. C. Zaehner in *Zen, Drugs and Mysticism*, pointed out at the time,

> Much of the attraction of Zen Buddhism to the 'drop-out' youth of today lies in its alleged spontaneity. Nothing could be further from the truth. For the achievement of Zen enlightenment an apprenticeship of grueling toil is the indispensable prerequisite. The late Professor

D. T. Suzuki, whose main concern was to present Zen to the West as attractively as possible, was largely responsible for minimizing the hardness of the Zen way.[30]

While this may be an accurate assessment of the effect Suzuki's Zen preaching had on some, it was certainly not Suzuki's intention to create a ready-fit mystic justification for demi-monde social degeneracy. And yet, the awkward question remains: on what grounds was he to judge the satoris of others, that most personal and individual of experiences and knowledge. This became particularly an issue when many mid-twentieth-century artists and intellectuals started equating satori with the sensation of consciousness-expansion induced by hallucinogenic drugs.

Aldous Huxley's Thought-Experiment Drug

In his book *The Doors of Perception*, Aldous Huxley talks about his experiences with hallucinogenic drugs. He describes how at one point when under the influence of mescaline he could suddenly understand perfectly a koan he "had read in one of Suzuki's essays." He remarks, "it had been, when I read it, only a vaguely pregnant piece of nonsense. Now it was all as clear as day, as evident as Euclid."[31] This statement by Huxley presents a tricky philosophical challenge to Suzuki's Zen. (And forget here about the argument that drugs may be socially and individually harmful, it is not relevant to the discussion.) If I take a pill and it gives me an experience that I feel (and hence "know") to be satori, and I can prove it by understanding koans, can I then declare myself to have become enlightened just the same as any other Zen master? If satori is self-validating, as Suzuki claimed it to be, this does present a conundrum. By extension, it raises the question, can satori be reduced to material sensations in the brain? Suzuki's response to Huxley's linking of his experience to Zen was one of complete dismissal. He outlined his views in an essay he wrote on the subject, translated as "Religion and Drugs."[32] He grounded his retort by referring, once again, to Lin-chi's key concept of the "True Man." He explained that "the aim of religion has to do with the *true man* himself, and not with the phenomenal world which is objectively experienced by the *man*."[33] In other words, we must remember that satori, and Zen knowledge as such, cannot reside in any subject or object. The problem with hallucinogenics, or any other form of neurological manipulation, is that although they may lead to feelings of an expanded consciousness or other sensations, these experiences are still dependent on a subject relating to the objective world and knowing this world as a subject. In fact, not only is the subject still there, but also the subject becomes entrapped by the objective world, experiencing a loss of will and freedom. "Aren't they like sleepwalkers?" remarks Suzuki.[34] This is the important distinction. Satori should not entail any loss of living will. The *true man* is there, right there, in the flesh. Lin-chi's statement was "There is the true man of no rank in the mass of naked flesh, who goes in and out form you facial gates [i.e., sense organs]. Those who have not yet testified [to the fact], look, look!"[35]

The key point to satori, and where it differs to expanded consciousness, meditation, trances, and so on, is that no loss of will is implied. It is not a passive surrender to the objective world, a discarding of conscious knowledge for dreamy states where one just moves without intention. Such states of mind involve losing one's will and freedom. Satori and Zen are not at all about this. As Suzuki writes:

> The teaching of the Buddha may now be summed up as follows: Seeing things thus or 'yathābhūtam' is the same as the attainment of perfect spiritual freedom; or we may say that when we are detached from evil passions based upon the wrong idea of selfhood and when the heart grows conscious of its own emancipation, we are then for the first time fully awakened to the truth as it really is. These two events, seeing and being freed, are mutually dependent, so intimately that the one without the other is unthinkable, is impossible; in fact they are two aspects of one identical experience, separated only in our limited cognition.[36]

This is one of the most essential arguments Suzuki is making about Zen knowledge. *To know is to be free.* This is not simple sloganeering. It is not a call for consciousness-raising about those things in the world that restrict your freedom. It is not calling on subjects to be aware of the objects out there in the world that bind them. In such an understanding, where subject and object are separate, so too is knowledge and freedom. In such cases, to know does not make you free, nor does it make you unfree. They are simply two different things. Of course, knowing, relative knowing as a subject, can be a step on the road to freedom, relative freedom, for the subject. If I awake and see that I am chained, at least I now know I am unfree and can do something about it. But with the absolute freedom that satori grants, it is as though the moment I know I am chained is the moment the chains dissolve and I am free. Knowing arises with the freedom. This is the world of the True Person beyond subject and object. It is an absurdity that can only be explained through analogies or metaphors (like my one just now about chains disappearing as soon as you know they are there). It makes no sense in the dualist world but makes all the sense in the world in satori. Which means that I should now just quote here another uncannily relevant koan. Here we go:

> When Kao was still a novice and not yet fully ordained, he came to Yao-shan.
> Yao-shan said, "Whence comest thou?"
> "From Nan-yüeh, sir."
> "Whiter goest though?"
> "To Chiang-ling for ordination."
> "What is your idea in getting ordained?"
> "I wish to be free from birth-and-death."
> "Do you know," said the master, "there is one who, even without being ordained, is free from birth-and-death?"[37]

Soku-hi Logic

Is the world innately illogical, as the koans seem to show us? The answer Suzuki would give is that formal logic is an act of bracketing off one part of reality from the whole, and in that context it works. But to attain a logic that describes the whole, that is, the world and you in it with your consciousness of here and now, we need to embrace a logic that is seemingly illogical but closer to the absolute truth than any traditional logical description can attain. This is where we come to Suzuki's concept of *soku-hi logic*, literally, "it is and it is not logic." The idea of soku-hi logic is that the law of identity must be shattered for ultimate truth to be expressed. A basic and conventional assumption we make about the world is that if there is an object or event A, then that object or event is A, and not something else, like B or non-A. This pen here is this pen, it is not that pencil over there. Once we maintain this law of identity the universe is coherent and meaningful and rational and logical. If this pen becomes that pencil over there we have entered the realm of magic, fantasy, irrationality, and madness. So how can Suzuki sustain his soku-hi logic logically and rationally. Again, it is all to do with the world without subject and object distinction. This is a world where objects are no longer clearly organized in a world out there by a subject. The world is just there and there are no objects in it. But there are also *no* no objects in it either. The world hasn't disappeared or been squeezed together into a crude monist mush. The fact that there is no subject means that there is nothing from which objects can disappear. Everything is given its thereness when the discerning subject is dissolved. Everything is existing as it is, *sonomama* (そのまま as it is), but because nothing is being gazed upon by a subject that has split itself off from the world, no objects are being granted a permanent essence sustained by the laws, or even conventions, of identity. When there is no subject or object the law of identity, or law of noncontradiction, or law of excluded middle simply does not operate. It would be like applying 3-D descriptions to a 2-D plain. One has to invent a depth that is not really there except in a delusional gaze.

Zen philosophy embraces two contradictory concepts for the very reason that they are contradictory. One is the idea of *emptiness*. The other is the idea of *thereness*. All is there and all is not there. This is what happens when subject and object drop away. Logically it means that A is A implies A is not A, therefore A is A. It is important that emptiness never implies that all disappears, and thereness never implies that everything is essentially existing as it is. One point about soku-hi logic is that it is not an attempt to explain the "dialectics" of the world, the fact that everything comes and goes through the course of time—as soon as a leaf appears it will turn brown as the unceasing cycle of life and death goes on with nothing ever enjoying permanency. No, this is not what soku-hi logic is describing. There is no time in the logic of soku-hi, the logic of Lin-chi's True Person in the here and now with subject and object being there or not being there being something of no consequence. There is no time for things to come and go. There isn't space either for them to come or go to. There is just here and now, thereness and emptiness. Is-ness and isn't-ness. Soku-hi.

Such assertions of contradiction and paradox may seem to many shallow and coy, involving nothing more than using words to produce ideas that fly in the face of common sense. But this is precisely the point that Suzuki wishes to make: language, logic, and formal philosophy cannot explain and express what is known in satori. Try to think again about those moments when you experienced the inklings of satori, when your mind accidently shoved you out of your common sense reality and you stood there in awe at your own existence in the world? Could you have put into words what was going on in your mind, your insights and knowledge during the moment it was happening? (If so, you are not remembering hard enough. Try again.) The point is that what you know, really know, as in become aware of in that sudden way, that you are here now in the world, is never like knowing any other fact in the world. It is not actually a fact in the world. There is no world and no you when it overtakes you. All that is left is a willed and willing knowledge coming from the you that is always just there.

Is Satori Meaningful?

Science and reason offer partial knowledge, which is also meaningful knowledge because it informs us of what our world is like and offers us creative explanations of the events we experience. Science and reason chart patterns in our reality and tell us *stories* about our world. For a story to work, the law of identity has to be maintained. A story must have stand-alone contrastive parts as it moves forward through time and narrative. Take for instance, the Gandavyūha Sutra from which I quoted earlier. It is indeed a story about identities that were assumed to have been separate but found to be one. Beatrice Suzuki (Suzuki's wife) summarized it as follows:

> In this Sutra Sudhana (善財) is the chief figure who inspired by Mañjuśri goes through a long pilgrimage … He finally comes to Maitreya (彌勒), the last of the long series of fifty-three teachers, each of whom has given him enlightening instructions according to his or her spiritual insight. Maitreya after teaching the pious pilgrim in religion advises him to go back to Mañjuśri … When he thinks of Mañjuśri with singleness of heart, the Bodhisattva suddenly appears to him … Sudhana, here throughout depicted as a youth seeking the light of truth, is no less than a manifestation of Mañjuśri himself, who, through the instructions of Maitreya, the future Buddha, now enters upon the path of spiritual life, which is love and wisdom.[38]

Sudhana is sent by Mañjuśri on a pilgrimage, only to discover that he is Mañjuśri himself. Sudhana was Mañjuśri all along. Wow! What was seen as different and separate was actually the same. The story would seem to conform to a soku-hi vision, A is not A and A is A. And yet to tell the story it is necessary to have one part where A is clearly not A, (Sudhana and Mañjuśri relate to each other as separate identities) and a follow-up part where A is clearly A (Sudhana discovers he is Mañjuśri). Otherwise, the story simply would not make any sense, to the extent that it would not be a "story" but rather random words on a page. Similarly, science must have its stories of how things work. If rocket engineers failed to see the essentialized dualistic distinction between hydrogen tanks and oxygen tanks this would seriously impede a rocket's chances of getting to the moon. Formal logic and the rational law of identity and non-contradiction enable us to know our world and tell our stories about it. Stories depend on a there and then contrasting with the here and now. In other words, what gives meaning to this world is not the raw data of the senses but a sense that everything we see and experience is within a wider situation and that situation is linked to a stream of meaning that we can call a narrative. When we experience something truly meaningless and absurd (a surprisingly rare occurrence in our lives, when you think about it) we feel it to be so because it has slipped out from all of our narratives. It stands alone, unlinked, unexplainable, and inexpressible. It cannot be made into a story.

Behind the diurnal narratives we use to make sense of our everyday situations will be one grand narrative, our cosmology, which is the story we hold to explain to ourselves absolutely everything. Most people's cosmology will be a story with a purpose, a teleology. Every trivial moment in our lives is part of one big picture that will make sense to us someday. The crisis of modern times, for many (at least within academia) has been the loss of this teleological narrative. Rather, there is the less joyful cosmology that the world appeared unintended due to unconscious natural forces. The story is that you are part of a cosmic machine. It is not there for any reason. And neither are you. This new cosmology has sparked off the whole trend of existential nihilism, people striving to find meaning when all is meaningless.[39] Of course, every religion rejects this nihility as every religion has a teleological cosmology, a story of why it is meaningful that the world was created as it is, even if that meaning is not always transparent.

But what of Zen? It is a religion, but does it have a teleology? Zen has no ultimate and final interest in the goings on out there in the world. All our stories are contrived in the eyes of Zen. Every story is entangled in the delusion that we are actors with selves having adventures in a world of people and objects that was designed by a God/author. There is no self. There are no objects. There is no author. There is just here and now in absolute emptiness. Is Zen, then, the ultimate (and perhaps only) existentially nihilistic religion around? The Zen rejection of our narratives is not based on the idea that they are absurd or hallucinations, but simply on the grounds that any story will only be one story out of an infinity of versions. The Zen aim is to hear that infinity of all possible stories from which the small few of conscious everyday stories emerge. In other words, rather than seeing the world as meaningless, Zen sees it as so meaningful that no one cosmology could ever explain it. Zen is the story before all stories. As such, it does not contradict or reject the stories of religion as, for example, atheism does. It just stands apart from them, watching both their narrative and its construction all at once. Zen sees both the movie and the DVD player at the same time, to use a perhaps less than profound analogy. Again, once more we assert that Zen is based on a knowledge that just happens. It is not a constructed argument, a hypothesized explanation, an imagined story, nor a considered account of things. It is a knowledge that has an absolute certainty about itself that does not go away, even if you were to will it to go away. The world is meaningful to us already even before we make stories about it. This meaning comes from the knowledge of the here and now which is an event for the "true man of no title," the selfless self, or the Unborn self. Here is Zen master Bankei (1622–1693), as quoted by Suzuki, explaining the significance of our already knowing the world before we come to know it.

> When you were coming this way to hear my sermon, or when you are actually listening to it, suppose you hear a bell or a crow. You at once recognize that the bell is ringing or the crow is crying, and you do not make any mistake. It is the same with your seeing; you pay no special attention to a certain thing, but when you see it you at once know what is what. It is the Unborn in you that works these miracles, and as long as you are all like that, you cannot deny the Unborn, which is the Buddha-mind, bright and illuminating.[40]

Zen Wisdom versus Philosophy

It can be agreed that science and reason only ever offer fragments of absolute truth. To offer the whole would be impossible as it would involve telling an infinite of stories all together in a single instant, something that is completely unthinkable in every sense of the term. Zen wisdom, on the other hand, is absolute since it is not extracting a narrative from a whole, but is suddenly, without narrative, grasping the whole in itself in its thusness in an emptiness that excludes nothing. Zen wisdom is complete, a vision of eternity from the standpoint of nothing, while science and reason, including philosophy, is only ever jumping from standpoint to standpoint. However, there is an argument to be made that in being so absolute, Zen wisdom ends up missing everything and grasping nothing. One philosopher who had problems with Suzuki's constant denigration of philosophy was the fellow Kyoto School philosopher Tanabe Hajime.[41]

Tanabe famously fell out with his erstwhile teacher and mentor Nishida Kitaro when Tanabe wrote an essay critical of Nishida titled, "*Requesting the Guidance of Professor Nishida*" in 1930. The details of Tanabe's criticism of Nishida are complicated and mostly not relevant here. But one point of interest for us is his view that Nishida's espousal of the (very Zen) notion of a "standpoint without a standpoint"[42] cannot be purported to be a form of wisdom superior to philosophy since it operates by leaving out other standpoints, becoming, in effect, a soteriological short-circuiting that is anathema to philosophy. Philosophy has to work with the mess of multiple standpoints. To adopt the standpoint of no standpoints would be to kill philosophy for the sake of a standpoint that does not seek to account for itself.

The general point being made is that the absolute wisdom of Zen is too pure to be of value in accounting for why our knowledge is impure to begin with. In other words, Zen offers wisdom and knowledge as a finished product and ignores the path and process it takes to get to wisdom. This is no small matter since a wisdom that excludes its own path cannot account for that path and hence remains an impoverished form of wisdom compared to those other forms of wisdom, in particular philosophy, which take their own path to be the grounds of their standpoint. To explain, let me give here a rough parable that I hope won't sound too corny. Zen wisdom is like walking into a dark room and suddenly turning on the light. All at once all that was unknown is now known in one instant. However, philosophy is like walking into a dark room, suddenly turning on the light, and then proceeding to walk around the room looking at everything from different angles. In doing so, the great wisdom you will discover is not what is in the room but the fact that you can never find one absolute angle from which to survey all that is to be found in the room. Your vision depends on where you stand meaning that no standpoint can be absolute (unless it claims, indeed, to be "a standpoint without a standpoint"). That is the finding of philosophy that an absolute satori cannot grasp. Understanding the absolute is easy, it is understanding the non-absolute that is hard.

Do Koans Demonstrate the Point They Are Not Trying to Make?

But what exactly is being left out of this satori experience, as Suzuki describes it? For one, it is the stories of our world and our lives. To tell a story, as I have said, bracketing reality, that is, chopping it up into separate bits, is needed. We must pick out objects and people and describe these and only these, ignoring inconsequential details. To avoid doing so would create an incoherent narrative. But, and here is a further complication, even an incoherent narrative involves bracketing and hence is, despite itself, engaging in coherence. Any text that is a text, and not just squiggles on a page, will run in a string of words and move in a line. The twentieth century has seen writers try and defy this line. One case, for example, would be William Burroughs and Brion Gysin who cut up texts making the strings of writing appear physically all over the page. Here is their own description of the process and motivation.

> Take a letter you have written or a letter written to you. Cut the page into four or into three columns—any way you may choose. Shuffle the pieces and put them together at random. Cut through the word lines to hear a new voice off the page. A dialogue often breaks out. "It" speaks. Herrigel describes such an experience in *Zen in the Art of Archery* when "It" shot the arrow.[43]

Similarly, other writers have sought to defy the linear sense of grammar producing texts that are words and even sentences but which make no sense. Here is an example from literature Nobel Prize winner Bob Dylan's novel *Terantula*: "Phombus Pucker. with his big fat grin. his hole in the head. his matter of fact knowledge of zen firecrackers. his little white lies. his visions of sugar plums. his dishwater hands."[44] What on earth does all that mean? And what are "zen firecrackers" by the way?

Of course, the Zen koan has always, *avant la lettre,* explored and revealed what the twentieth-century's literati later came to know, that language's linearity is a construct that can be destroyed in an utterance. But the problem with all these experiments in non-linear irrational language is that they reveal that writing depends not on writers, or texts, but on readers. When someone presents me with a cut-up text, I still read it linearly. I will even cock my head to the side to do so if I have to. When Helene Cixous wrote a parallel bilingual text called *Vivre l'orange* with French on one side and English on the other, the presence of two texts in one was something that many commentators found intriguing. Sharon Willis, for example, wrote: "How can I read this text? Is it, in its originary bilingualness, accessible only to the bilingual reader, since one is constantly suspended between the two languages? How can I read it? Where does it address me, in English or in my French? … Who is the reader? Possibly the one who inhabits and is inhabited by both languages, at the border between them."[45] It is a fair question. But the answer really though is that when reading a bilingual text you probably read a bit of the text in one language and then a bit of the text in the other language. There is no mystery to it and language learners, for example, do it all the time. We humans, alas, just do not have the physical capacity to read cut up or parallel or deconstructed text in the non-linear multivocal way the post-moderns want us to. They want us to glide in a firmament of infinite interpretation when really we are on a lumbering train trapped between tracks of line by line reading.

Furthermore, not only do we always physically read by following one line of text, we humans also have a very bizarre ability to find meaning in the most meaningless of utterances. Koans (just like Dada art and other similar examples in history) reveal that attempts to destroy meaning just create it anew. Koans, once their initial shock value wore off, became part and parcel of English-speaking culture. Many, if not most, English speakers now know koans to be quaint little nuggets of irrationality that sparkle up exotic delights, like zen firecrackers in the night of reason. Even Suzuki himself tended to find meaning and coherence in koans. He harnessed koans as illustrative parables to emphasize points of Zen doctrine. Far from being random, they revealed, in Suzuki's telling, a pattern of profound sermonizing on Zen knowledge. For instance, there is a famous koan about Joshu's stone bridge. To paraphrase it briefly, a monk sees a log bridge which he had heard to be a stone bridge. He asks Joshu where the stone bridge is. Joshu tells him that the log bridge is the stone bridge. The monk is puzzled. Joshu says, "Horses go over it, asses go over it."[46] Suzuki, after recounting the koan remarks, "This seems to be but a trivial talk about a bridge, but considered from the inner way of looking at such cases, there is a great deal of truth touching the centre of one's spiritual life." He then interprets the stone bridge metaphorically to mean all of us in our daily life with the burdens of the world tramping over us. Suzuki adds, "was Jōshu referring to this kind of bridge? In any event we can read something of the sort in the cases above cited."[47] Note how Suzuki is reading "something" into this koan case. Like so many other commentators on Zen in modern times he just can't help himself from doing so. Koans, once they seeped out from beyond the walls of traditional Rinzai Zen temples have taken on new meanings and cultural coding in the wider English-speaking world which proves that language is never meaningless even when intended to be. This is not to say that koans are a mistake or a fraud but that they do have their context, in the spiritual practices and goals inside the confines of a Zen temple, and when this context is forgotten there is always the danger that koans will undermine the very point they want to make, that language does not signify everything. Of course, the obvious response to this is to say that the fact that koans can become so quickly normalized and ritualized by society demonstrates that we need even more newer and fresher koans constantly to keep us vigilant and free from the socially constructed *maya* (delusions) of language and discourse.

True Man and Straw Man

The fact that humans do tend to find meaning everywhere, indicates that non-dualistic knowledge is never really fully sustainable in social life. Humans crave meaning that is linear, that is narrative, that is about the over there and then, that is not stuck in the infinite circle of here and now. The Zen knowledge that Suzuki describes is a knowledge that comes ready-made all at once in one package. And, as we have seen, such knowledge is not actually informative. It is the knowledge that comes intuitively and instinctively to the most basic consciousnesses. Knowledge of an informative type involves conscious discovery, a road to greater wisdom willfully taken. Satori is either at the beginning or end of this journey but it can never present itself in the middle, arguably the most meaningful part. Suzuki's response, though, would be that linear knowledge and narrative is knowledge that is constructed which makes it always something removed from what is there. It is only the partial reflection of the actualness that can never be fully represented linearly, in one story. Philosophy has its place but it is a road that will never lead to wisdom but only run parallel to it. To reach wisdom one must eventually jump off it. But when one has jumped off the path of reason and philosophy and reached the absolute knowledge of satori where can you go from there?

Suzuki's criticism of philosophy and science was often made part and parcel of his more general criticism of what he saw as the Western way of thinking. The problem, in his view, is that Westerners, through philosophy and science, divide the world in two. Suzuki once remarked:

> As I always keep saying, Westerners think about things after they have divided everything in two. Easterners reflect back on before there is a division into two, in other words, before subject and object have

been divided. This is the basic way of thinking in the East. Westerners cannot think about anything without dividing it into two.[48]

Westerners are those who divide the world but do not understand that those divisions are accidental, that reality is more than labelled objects out there in the world. Westerners confuse their conscious recognition of an object with the object itself. Using an old Zen analogy, Suzuki was fond of accusing the rational West of confusing the finger that points at the moon with the moon itself. But at this point we do really need to interject and ask if Suzuki's accusations are in any way correct. Confusing the moon for the finger that points at it: would a Westerner ever really be dumb enough to do this? ("Is this the moon or the finger? I'm confused.") Not even in a state of extreme intoxication would this happen. Of course, Suzuki is most likely using this as a metaphor in the sense that Westerners confuse reality with the language we use to describe it. Again, my point still stands: are Westerners really that stupid? Would anyone ever confuse the word "dog" with the thing that runs around wagging its tail? Now, maybe Suzuki's point is that Westerners confuse abstract ideas with concrete reality. Again, this is accusing Westerners of gross idiocy. Whatever way we put it, I really do not believe that there are Westerners who consciously divide the world into subject and object all the time as Suzuki claims. I cannot even picture how this could be done. It would be the ultimate psychotic malfunction ("this is subject: that is object," "this is subject: that is object," "this is subject: that is object" ad infinitum). What Westerners do, though, is what everyone does, become aware of their situation and position when needs be. If a Westerner and an Easterner were to go rambling happily alone in a forest neither would be aware of any subject-object distinction. Unless they saw a wild boar coming charging at them. In which case they would. There is no obvious occident-orient divide in such matters.

But Suzuki's mistake is more than just getting carried away with clever sounding but slightly silly stereotypes. It is the fact that he is confusing the *conscious state* of not being aware at this moment of any subject and object with the Zen epistemological assertion, expressed in the concept of *emptiness*, that there is no *essential* subject and object. No subject-object division in your mind is not the same thing as emptiness. To understand this distinction, between not consciously dividing between subject and object and the condition of absolute emptiness, let us look at two central passages in Lin-chi's [Japanese: Rinzai] (-866) key work on Zen philosophy, the ninth-century *The Record of Linchi* [臨濟語錄]. The first one is when Lin-chi explicitly discusses this issue of states of consciousness in what is called the "Four Classifications." Lin-chi stated.

> Sometimes I take away the person but do not take away the surroundings; sometimes I take away the surroundings but do not take away the person; sometimes I take away both person and surroundings; sometimes I take away neither person nor surroundings.[49]

We have two elements here (*person* and *surroundings*) and four states created by whether the person or the surroundings has been taken away. Following the interpretation of the Japanese philosopher Izutsu Toshihiko (井筒俊彦 1914–1993), we can assume "person" to be the subject and "surroundings" to be object.[50] This makes sense as there is no other appropriate label to give them. The four states or conditions become subject but no object, object but no subject, subject and object together, no subject or object. Izutsu makes the further important point that these four categories do not represent a gradation, as in one state being better than the other.[51] Rather they come and go, not in any particular order. The second key passage from the *Record of Linchi* is the one I quoted early. I will quote it again here using a different translation.

> The Master ascended the hall and said, "Here in this lump of red flesh there is a True Man of no rank. Constantly he goes in and out the gates of your face. If there are any of you who don't know this for a fact, then look! Look!"
>
> At that time there was a monk who came forward and asked, "What is he like—the True Man with no rank?"
>
> The Master got down from his chair, seized hold of the monk and said, "Speak! Speak!"

The monk was about to say something, whereupon the Master let go of him, shoved him away, and said, "True Man with no rank—what a shitty ass-wiper!" The Master then returned to his quarters.[52]

Again, it is Izutsu who makes the crucial point that the four states happen separately to each other but all of them are connected with the True Person of No Rank. Which means that "person" as contrasted to "surroundings" is not to be confused with the "True Person." Suzuki makes the same distinction and connection in his commentary on the *Record of Linchi* called *Rinzainokihonshiso* 『臨済の基本思想』 (*The Basic Thought of Rinzai*).

> But the person here is not the *True Person*. It is the person confronting the surroundings so it is not the absolute or transcendent person. It is the limitation of the True Person, the representation of the True Person. The true person clearly at the foundation which has to be grasped in-between, it cannot be seen in the relationship and negotiation between person and surroundings, it is not mindful whether one or two has been removed or not removed.[53]

Suzuki goes on to interpret Lin-chi's insight as follows:

> The true person cannot be represented theoretically as something classifiable. The true person becomes the person and the surroundings, becomes the subject and the object, and unfolds in the world of one and many. In which case, human thinking moves in accordance with four particular forms. The surroundings are affirmed, and the person is negated, the surroundings are negated, and the person affirmed, both person and surroundings are both negated, both person and surroundings are affirmed. We can consider these four scenarios. The true person is theoretically reflected here we can naturally say. Rinzai merely wanted to say that as a theorist.[54]

To hammer home my argument let me quote from another Suzuki book, 『金剛経の禅』 (*Diamond Sutra Zen*) that makes the same point, that we should not confuse conscious states of subject and object with the ontology of the Zen True Person.

The world of person and surroundings divided is the world of general knowledge. Taking both away is an absolute negation of the world of differentiation. The negation is absolute but an absolute affirmation emerges and neither the person and the surroundings are taken away. In other words, the person stands as the person, the surroundings stand as the surroundings. The world of discrimination is there (sonomama) in equality, and equality is there (sonomama) in discrimination. This is the aim of Lin-chi.[55]

Sometimes there is the subject, sometimes there is the object, sometimes there is the subject and object, sometimes neither. This is the condition of everyone regardless of nationality. And Suzuki's interpretation here of Lin-chi's words supports this view, making his dualistic obsessions of supposed Western dualistic obsessionalism sound bizarre, un-Zen, and lacking in reason. It has to remain one of the wonders of twentieth-century intellectual history that Suzuki's shallow stereotyping of Westerners—those subject-object dividing simpletons—has been hailed by so many to be such a supreme sagacious insight.

Monist Tourism

I remember a few years ago visiting briefly with my daughter a rural Zen temple in Aichi Prefecture in Japan during a Sunday afternoon ramble in the countryside. Outside the temple, they had set up a simple canopy and a pleasant young lady, perhaps in her late teens or early twenties, was serving cups of tea to the random tourists, like myself and my little girl. While I sat there sipping the rich green tea, digging the dharma, I decided to ask her about the temple. Was it a Soto or Rinzai temple? Rinzai, she told me. I suggested then—flaunting my learning—that they must do lots of koans in there. She seemed unfamiliar with the word "koan," so I explained the characters to her ("ko" as in "public park," "an" as in "written proposal"—that is how you "spell" things in Japanese). She did not know the word. So I asked about mondo ("mon" as in "question." "do" as in "answer"). It is a common word, meaning "questions and answers," but she was not familiar with it in a Zen context. However, she did tell me that temple does have "seppou," a word I was not actually familiar with. (It means "sermons"—"sep-" as in "explanation" and "pou" as in "law.") The point of my anecdote is to show how Zen wisdom is not actually that big in Japan. Most people see Zen as simply their local provider of funeral services ("funeral Buddhism"—*soshiki-bukkyo*, as it is known) rather than the source and sanctuary of the prajñā-paramita philosophy of non-duality. There is nothing wrong with this. It is the very normal disconnect that will always exist between a religion's philosophy and its actual sociology in any country. However, the fact that so many Western intellectuals over the decades have assumed Zen to be something that all Japanese are *au fait* with, and indeed to be the everyday dynamic of Japanese consciousness and the base reference for all its cultural forms is thanks to the formidable powers of persuasion of D. T. Suzuki.

One such intellectual was Arthur Koestler who in 1956 took a trip to Japan to find out what wisdom this land of non-dualist exotica had to offer. The resulting book from this trip, *The Lotus and the Robot*, details his impressions of Japan (and India, which he also visited). Like so many books written about Japan, it contains constant outbursts of disbelief at the paradoxical mysteries of Japanese society. The book presents stereotypes aplenty of Japan, but it also functions, unintentionally, as a stereotype of Arthur Koestler himself, a hyper-intense, overlearned, dour, and chronically unrelaxed Mitel European intellectual overanalyzing and taking too seriously the frolics and frivolities of a foreign land.

To understand Japan, Koestler takes his cue from Ruth Benedict's famous book *The Chrysanthemum and the Sword* (1946). This work is from that popular mid- to late-twentieth-century genre that could be described as "pathological anthropology." It starts with the assumption that there is something wrong with Japan (they are not normal Americans) and then proceeds to work out why this is the case. The diagnosis Benedict comes up with is that the Japanese do not experience guilt. Whereas Americans experience both shame, that outer sense of social embarrassment, and guilt, that inner feeling that you have broken universal codes of moral law, the Japanese only feel shame. Koestler adopts this very suspect assumption unquestioningly and poses the opinion that for this reason Zen suits the Japanese very well since Zen is precisely the religion and philosophy than shuns any rational and universalizing metaphysics or ethics that could be the grounds for feeling guilty. Koestler goes on to describe Japan as a land where people live in strict quasi-Confucianist-style conformity and where, at the same time, they espouse a religion, Zen, that rejects all conventions. They are conformists and non-conformists at the same time. Oh! How paradoxical these mysterious Japanese be!

What we should note here is how Koestler's view of Japan has been so thoroughly shaped by D. T. Suzuki. Japan is the land of Zen, not one ounce of doubt about that for Koestler. However, while Koestler sees everything through Suzuki's Zen lens, the book ends up becoming quite a lengthy and explicit attack on Suzuki, often bordering on the insulting. Koestler takes very much a pathological approach during his tour of Japan's anthropological delights. He remarks of the Japanese that "what makes them into bleeders is the pathogenic discrepancy between the conditions under which they live, and the unattainable standards of perfection which they have been taught to apply to themselves, almost from their first outing in the mother's pouch."[56] The Japanese are just simply mad as hatters! It is as though Koestler is meeting Suzuki's slanderings of West with his own contumacies of the East. Whereas Suzuki obsessively saw Westerners as stuck in a mode where they must chronically divide the world into subject and object, Koestler is fixed on the notion that the Japanese are at the level always where subject and object are eternally one, with the result that people are zombified conformists, with the odd unfathomable and mad burst of creativity when the originality of Zen every so often punctures the Confucianist surface, something rare, and perhaps even impossible nowadays for rigidified contemporary Zen.

Suzuki wrote a lengthy response to Koestler titled "A Reply from D. T. Suzuki." He remarks of some Zen monks Koestler met on his tour, "why did they not give Mr. Koestler Rinzai's '*Kahtz!*' or Tokusan's stick and chase him out of the temple?"[57] The joke is rough but given that Koestler's criticisms of Suzuki were hard core ("I have always been puzzled by Dr. Suzuki's striking spiritual resemblance to either Tweedledum or Tweedledee, whose twin suchness are no doubt meant to symbolize ... the deluding or deluded mind"), this is understandable.[58] It isn't actually hard for Suzuki to counterattack, since Koestler has conformed ever so precisely to Suzuki's stereotypes of the West. He coolly observes once more that, "Westerners start with the distinction between subject and object. Zen goes beyond it, or wants us to see how they are before this distinction was introduced."[59] Koestler asks too many obtusely logical questions and misses the point of everything. He is a subject asking about an object, little knowing that the object is in the subject and the subject is in the object and to ask will ensure that you will never know this. Silly dualistic *auslander*!

Going back to Koestler's criticisms, one acerbic comment he makes about satori is that there seems to be "big satoris and little satoris." Unintentionally, this cynical remark is actually spot on. The fact is that satori is not something that can ever be quantified, qualified, or measured. Let us remember again what satori is, that absolute certain knowledge of one's own existence in the world in the here and now, a knowledge the awareness of which can only be experienced in the mind of an individual. It is not really beyond *all* description, just simply *consistent* description. As something individual, no individual will ever be able to fully represent it to anyone else. And so it will, to someone as category obsessive as Koestler, seem like a "rubbery concept."[60] This rubbery-ness, this fluidity, this vagueness, the fact that any analogy to describe what satori is will be describing also what it is not is exactly the power of satori conceptually. It also means that satori cannot be connected to the superficial, uninformative, and, in fact, weirdly meaningless issue of whether people in the East and West see always subjects or objects, or both, or neither. As Lin-chi said with his four classifications, seeing subject and object and both and neither comes and goes. And behind those comings and goings is the True Person without Rank. Note well that phrase: True Person *without rank*! It means that human consciousness, regardless of who, what, where, and how you are is where the person of no rank is at. This has to be one of the most profoundly humanistic concepts in all of religious history. It is heralding and celebrating at the purest level what unites all humans, explaining why we are, all of us, the walking sites of the divine infinite. Every single one of us is the person of no rank within. Think of those humans who are very different to you. Down the road from me, for example, there is a museum with ceramic jars made over four thousand years ago. I often stare at those jars and try to image the people whose hands made and used them. What went on in their minds? What were the dreams, aspirations, ideals, fears, angers, arguments, jokes, and passions of these people living in small hunter-gathering communities four millennia ago? No doubt very different to ours in so many hard to imagine ways. But one thing these people had in common with us was a human consciousness with its innate knowledge of existence in the here and now, a knowledge we are not always, and in fact very rarely, aware of but which is always there. (And let us remind ourselves again that knowing you are here and now without being aware of it is not a contradiction.) This is the glorious knowledge of satori. A message of individual sacredness and humanist togetherness. But, alas, Suzuki made a mess of the message and garbled its true meaning. In his row with Koestler he let the puerile delusions of the identity politics of his times, the *maya* of nationalism, warp his delivery. It made him sculpt the rubbery concept of satori into something as impenetrable as stone to be cast at those who were maybe culturally different but, as a Buddhist ought to know, humanly the same.

Zen in the Art of Whatever

Satori, as an inner awareness or awakening to the knowledge of the here and now, is something the description of which you either get or do not. As such, criticisms of it or doubts about it, such as those voiced by Koestler, will always bounce off it. However, it is on the issue of the *application* of Zen knowledge, as in the Zen of this and that, that Koestler is on stronger ground. He looks closely at the claims made in Herrigel's book on *Zen in the Art of Archery*. He feels that the esoteric descriptions given by Herrigel of learning kendo are exaggerated ways of expressing something that is common place and not exclusively to be found in Zen.

Basically, when you practice something often enough, you will do it automatically. Zen, for Koestler, is combining two psychological truisms: that we often do things automatically in a brilliant way when we learn it enough, and, that the human mind has the ability to create spontaneously new associations between things that are conventionally separate. We are both patterned and unpredictable. Zen psychology pushes for both tendencies, but in doing so it is not particularly evoking any special knowledge, just commonplace folk psychology. Interestingly, in a later book he wrote, *The Act of Creation*, Koestler describes human behavior as occurring within strict matrices, with occasional sudden creative awakenings, as we can call them, occurring when a leap is made in the mind between these separate matrices. To illustrate patterned automatic behavior, Koestler mentions piano playing, "A bar-pianist can perform in his sleep or while conversing with the barmaid: he has handed control to the automatic pilot as it were."[61] The piano player in this case could say that he is not playing but (Herrigel-style) "It" plays. Koestler's point, in the *Lotus and the Robot*, is that Zen arts are just regular arts, the same as for example playing the piano, and specifying them to be "Zen" and hence a product of a special type of knowledge is overselling Zen.

The fact that Koestler provides an alternative non-Zen hypothesis (about matrices in his book *The Act of Creation*) to explain exactly the same inner psychological phenomena that Zen explains does not, of itself, prove invalid the claims of Zen. And, indeed, there is good reason to suppose that Zen's message of non-duality will always be words of wisdom to those aiming to accomplish perfect practice in their chosen field. However, it does highlight how Zen as the path to the absolute knowledge of satori, and Zen as a technique for better concentration when performing a given art, are two separate things. And in linking the knowledge of satori to the knowledge of a practitioner in a chosen art, Suzuki was arguably downgrading satori from the knowledge of the person without rank to the knowledge of a person with a rank in a particular sport or art.

Suzuki can argue that the Zen arts are the application of satori. The knowledge of your oneness with the world can inform and inspire you to really become one with the world in terms of actions and poise, by helping diminish distracting conscious subject and object awareness. There is satori and there is the application of satori which, although it may mirror the psychological insights of secular psychology, is nevertheless built on knowledge of a different source. This is all fine, but it does mean that Suzuki has to allow for Zen to be found in those arts and practices that are not traditionally Zen, such as piano playing and motorcycle maintenance. This raises the question of whether Zen is a neutral platform from which all games can be played or whether Zen is specific only to certain cultural codings. This issue will be discussed further in the next chapter.

World

Culture, Value, Belief

What are the beliefs and doctrines of Zen? There are none. Zen is about the here and now, the True Person of No Rank, the consciousness when mind and body drop away. Such a thing could never have beliefs or doctrines. To assume it had such things (Suzuki will argue) would be to misunderstand from the very beginning what it is. However, while Zen may not have *beliefs* it does have a *culture*. Or rather, Zen is manifest in certain cultural activities. The problem, as I hope to demonstrate, is that to have a culture is to have beliefs. A culture, what we do habitually, is based upon value (what we consider to be beautiful or not) and values (what we consider to be acceptable or not). And these are in turn connected to beliefs since beliefs are, by definition, the consistent understandings and justifications we give to our values and sense of value. *Culture, value,* and *belief*—Social scientists may argue over which shapes which but either way, they are all linked and we can follow the connections between them. Zen is no different. In the following sections, let's start with Zen culture and work from there to Zen values, and from there on to Zen beliefs. The core point here is that the absolute freedom of Zen in the here and now will also always have a discernable form. As Suzuki explains.

> While Zen teaching consists in grasping the spirit by transcending form, it unfailingly reminds us of the fact that the world in which we live is a world of particular forms and that the spirit expresses itself only by means of form. Zen is, therefore, at once antinomian and disciplinarian.[1]

Antinomian and disciplinarian: spontaneity made rigid and rigidity made spontaneous. The intriguing tensions in such a belief system are already obvious.

Zen Culture

One of Suzuki's most influential books has been *Zen and Japanese Culture*, which was originally published in more or less the same form in 1938 under the title *Zen Buddhism and Its Influence on Japanese Culture*. As these titles suggest, the book looks at the influence Zen has had in Japanese culture. By "culture" Suzuki means various arts and practices found in traditional Japan, namely, tea ceremony, haiku poetry, ink paintings, and swordsmanship. The trick to reading the book is to switch off your inner critical voice and just surrender to its romantic nationalist fantasies. Enjoy its alluring descriptions of an ataraxic arcadia, a serene land where stillness, silence, and serenity ripples through the hearts of its gentle people. I do not intend here to break this fantasy, and after all social realism, the assumption that everyone in a society is miserable, can also be a fiction. Rather, my aim is to use Suzuki's description of Zen culture to chart his underlying Zen values and beliefs. Suzuki is clear that what is to be seen in the arts and culture of the Japanese is the Zen way of seeing the world, that is Zen values (my word) which celebrate an intuitive mind (Suzuki's word).

> There is truth in the saying that the Oriental mind is intuitive while the Western mind is logical and discursive. An intuitive mind has its weaknesses, it is true, but its strongest point is demonstrated when it deals with things most fundamental in life, that is, things related to religion, art, and metaphysics. And it is Zen that has particularly established this fact—in *satori*. The idea that the ultimate truth of life and of things generally is to be intuitively and not conceptually grasped, and that this intuitive apprehension is the foundation not only of philosophy but of all other cultural activities, is what the Zen form of Buddhism has contributed to the cultivation of artistic appreciation among the Japanese people.[2]

Let us consider the tea ceremony or *cha-no-yu*. This is an old art or practice whereby a small group of people gather in a tea-hut and drink green tea that has been prepared before them in a fairly ritualistic way, by which I mean that certain actions when making the tea (where to put your hands, how to position the spoon, and so on) are done in a prescribed way. The tea-ceremony is very closely associated with Zen, in that it was introduced into Japan through Zen connections and those who have theorized about tea ceremony in the past have done so through Zen terms and concepts. For Suzuki, the tea ceremony is linked to Zen because it promotes stillness in behavior and refrainment from excitement and excess movement. This kind of introvertedness, Suzuki tells us, is more in keeping with Zen than the garrulousness one associates with alcohol, such as to be found in the wine-drinking culture of Christianity.[3] We can also gather that Zen approves formal ritualized behavior. Formality and stillness are connected to the Zen idea that the mind is distracted in its everyday world and needs to lose these distractions to become conscious once more in a non-dualistic way. As Suzuki sums it up,

> We can see now that the art of tea is most intimately connected with Zen not only in its practical development but principally in the observance of the spirit that runs through the ceremony itself. The spirit in terms of feeling consists of "harmony" (*wa*), "reverence" (*kei*), "purity" (*sei*), and "tranquility" (*jaku*).[4]

Looking at poetry, we can also see that Zen art is very much about minimalism in expression. The working principle of less words the better makes haikus more appropriately Zen than, say, epics. Why is less better? This is linked to the Zen idea that truth and reality are in the here and now and awareness of this is awareness of the great mystery that underlies it in what is termed *myo* by Suzuki.[5] The *haiku* poem must aim to stick to the here and now in which this *myo* is seen and known. We are to avoid creating more and more divisions with our words and the concepts they represent since that brings us further away from the initial intuitive spark of spiritual inspiration from which our creative act oozed up.

All things come out of an unknown abyss of mystery, and through every one of them we can have a peep into the abyss. You do not have to compose a grand poem of many hundred lines to communicate the feelings thus awakened by looking into the abyss. When a feeling reaches its highest pitch, we remain silent, because no words are adequate. Even seventeen syllables may be too many. In any event, Japanese artists, more or less influenced by the way of Zen, tend to use the fewest words or strokes of the brush to express their feelings. When feelings are too fully expressed, no room is left for the unknown, and from this unknown start the Japanese arts.[6]

We must not generate more bytes of information that will warp and garble forever the zero byte of the mysterious unknown. Zen poetry and painting also demonstrate a deep appreciation of scenes of nature. Again, we are seeing the values of thereness, appreciating the world as it naturally occurs as presented to us when we submit to just seeing it. There is an avoidance of too much detail, but also too much narrative. There are just random scenes as they are, and as they linger impressionistically.

And then there is the art of swordsmanship, an appreciation for which Suzuki was filled with excited enthusiasm and for which his legacy has taken a battering in subsequent years. Swordsmanship is an art in the sense that it involves techniques that can be done well, even ascetically, with training. Note, for instance, how fencing is an Olympic sport. As with the tea ceremony and archery, swordsmanship can be done with complete spontaneous naturalness when practiced enough. A trained swordsman will just move without any conscious planning or deliberation. The connection to Zen is the concept of *mushin* or no-mindedness. As we have seen, Zen Buddhism subscribes to the notion that there are two minds going on in any moment (but of course, one mind encompasses the other so there are never really two minds). There is the mind of conscious decision-making, deciding what to do. And then there is the mind of no-mind, the mind that sees and knows the here and now and moves as one with all the world. In other words, the true art of swordsmanship, when the swordsman moves with all the naturalness of the wind, mirrors the psychology of Zen, the idea that our mind is ultimately no-mind since our actions are fused with the world in a codependent arising. This, of course, we have already explored in the preceding chapters.

Suzuki wrote all this in his 1938 book *Zen Buddhism and its Influence on Japanese Culture.* The book was written in English and well received.[7] The West has always had bit of a love affair with the samurai, those swashbuckling heroes who impart in somber and humorless tones words of Bushido wisdom as they whack and slash their enemies with acrobatic precision. In 1900, Nitobe Inazō (新渡戸稲造 1862–1933) wrote, in English, the book *Bushido: The Soul of Japan* to great acclaim in the west. The killing function of the samurai was of no concern to its occidental readers. Okakura Kakuzō (岡倉覚三 1863–1913) in his book *The Book of Tea,* also written in English, in 1906 chastises the west for this, arguing that when Japan was closed off to the world and attacking no one it was condemned as barbaric. But when it won a vicious war against Russia it was hailed as being most advanced. Instead of samurai and their swords, Okakura preferred to promote the art of tea:

> [A westerner] was wont to regard Japan as barbarous while she indulged in the gentle arts of peace: he calls her civilised since she began to commit wholesale slaughter on Manchurian battlefields. Much comment has been given lately to the Code of the Samurai,—the Art of Death which makes our soldiers exult in self-sacrifice; but scarcely any attention has been drawn to Teaism, which represents so much of our Art of Life.[8]

Okakura, unlike Suzuki, did realize that the tea ceremony and swordsmanship were not at all similar activities, one being obviously very much more violent and horrible than the other. By the time Suzuki was writing his peon to the sword hacking ways of the samurai the international situation had changed considerably and Japan's overseas wars were not now seen in such benign terms compared to the turn of the century. In light of what we know now about the war in China in the 1930s, Suzuki's blasé prose is of course disturbing. Introducing the old Bushido text *Hagakure* he comments, "There is a document recently talked very much about in connection with the military operations in China."[9] We know now how awful these "operations" were. Another unnerving comment appears at the end of his chapter on "Zen and the Samurai" where he drags Zen into the quagmire of Japan's wars at that time.

> The Japanese hate to see death met irresolutely and lingeringly; they desire to be blown way like the cherries before the wind, and no doubt this Japanese attitude toward death must have gone very well with the teaching of Zen. The Japanese may not have any specific philosophy of life, but they have decidedly one of death, which may sometimes appear to be that of recklessness. The spirit of the samurai deeply breathing Zen into itself propagated its philosophy even among the masses. The latter, even when they are not particularly trained in the way of the warrior, have imbibed his spirit and are ready to sacrifice their lives for any cause they think worthy. This has repeatedly been proved in the wars Japan has so far had to go through.[10]

There has been much debate in recent years about Suzuki's writings and attitude during the Second World War. Brian Victoria in his book *Zen and War,* published in 1997, pointed out how various Zen leaders actively supported the War. His book also included quotes from Suzuki, such as the ones I have used above, to make the charge that Suzuki was sympathetic to some extent to militarism at this point in his career.[11] But Suzuki has had his defenders ranging from those who have either minimized Suzuki's seemingly pro-war comments to those who have gone as far as to say that Suzuki was a staunch opponent of the war and militarism.[12] Victoria wrote as an active member of the Zen religion and, as such, he is entitled to make the criticisms he made. In fact, his book has done Zen great favors by bringing these issues out into the open. Religions do badly when they ignore or hide past mistakes. (And Zen is a religion—thinking your religion is not a religion is always the first mistake a religion will make.) But from a secular scholarly point of view, does Suzuki have a case to answer? To the charge that he was a militarist, defined as someone who believed that the military had a supreme role in Japanese society and that Japan had a moral mission to conquer its neighbors, the answer is, I believe, no. Suzuki did on occasion explicitly criticize the military and what they were doing, for instance in 1944, when it was quite risky, he was heard at a public talk to condemn the formation of kamikaze squads.[13] Sure, there are other quotations, such as the ones above, that seem to present a different attitude, but if Suzuki had truly been pro-militarism this would have been made completely obvious in his voluminous writings. The fact that the only evidence is patchy and selective quotes exonerates him. However, I think also it is an exaggeration to go to the other extreme and claim that he was actively opposed to the War. This is not completely true either. The War happened and he accepted that it was happening, and that this was the situation that Japan, through bad decisions, rather than innately immoral ideologies, had fallen into. In a comment shortly after the war, Suzuki stated that in regard to incidents such as the Manchurian Incident, "To tell the truth, people like myself were just not very interested in such things."[14] It may sound surprising that he could have been so indifferent to events, but it is probably quite an accurate statement of Suzuki's wartime experiences. I personally think we should take Suzuki's word for it, that the war was something that went on far away from his daily concerns. His words should be seen through the eyes of historians, rather than moralists, as an informative account of just how complicated, contradictory, and, for contemporary readers, incomprehensible domestic reaction was at the time to Japan's military adventures abroad. However, while I think Suzuki is not guilty of militarism, it is obvious that he was an incurable Japanese ethno-nationalist. This is not a sin in itself, but, as I have argued previously, it did warp his understanding of Zen leading him to miss his own point about the non-dualism of prajñā philosophy and how the True Person of No Rank should also be the True Person of No Nationality. As Suzuki never failed to point out, Zen Buddhism is all about overcoming your delusions and attachments. It seems that at times Suzuki did not listen to his own message. Furthermore, his fixation on swordsmanship and his stark and astonishing inability, unlike Okakura, to see any particular difference between killing someone with a sword and drinking a cup of tea, exposes the further problem of Zen ethics—if there are actually any at all.

But before looking at questions of ideologies and ethics, I wish to sum up the connections we have made between Zen culture and its values and beliefs. The arts of Zen, or rather, those arts that have been heavily influenced by Zen, reveal that Zen values stillness, ritualized movement, minimalism in artistic representation, and nature over narrative. These styles of behavior or artistic expression are favored because they are in-keeping with Zen beliefs, which I think can be fairly summarized by the concepts of *non-duality*, *emptiness*, and *thereness*. Now, Suzuki told us that Zen does not have beliefs but it seems that it does, and its arts and culture, by Suzuki's own description, reveal these. Suzuki may respond that what I am describing as Zen beliefs are not "beliefs" but just awareness of things as they are. When I see the rain fall I do not believe the rain is falling, it just simply is falling. Fine. But if Zen is simply everything is as it is, why is not absolutely every act of culture or artistic expression not an act of Zen? Why are haikus more Zen-like than a thousand lines of epic verse? Why are minimalist ink painting more Zen than the fauvist mannerist styles of *ukiyo-e* prints? And why is it more Zen to brandish a sword than to throw a bomb (or even better, throw down your sword and make a peace sign with your fingers)? It is because Zen is valuing something. It is ranking the world's arts and cultural patterns. It is perfectly acceptable and normal for it to do this, but in doing so, it cannot also claim to be not doing it. It cannot claim to be a religion with no beliefs or values when it very evidently has these in abundance.

Style for or from Zen?

There is also a further issue here of what exactly is the cause-effect relationship between Zen and Zen art. Does the experience of Zen really produce Zen art or are they two separate things? All the major world religions have particular artistic styles and traditions associated with them. We can talk of Islamic, Christian, and Buddhist art. When it comes to the contents of those arts the link is often completely obvious, such as in paintings of religious scenes, or statues of Buddha. When it comes to choice of style, form, and more general content, the link is not so obvious. An art form may arise within a certain religious community but how much is the religion actually shaping the art? Often times the connection between the two is an assumption that seems obvious after the fact simply because the two occurred together: correlation, not cause relation. Let me explain this with a simpler example relating art to politics (and please bear with me here). In the 1980s, the British pop group *Duran Duran* was considered by many musical journalists to be producing music that was "Thatcherite." However, let us suppose that Margret Thatcher had lost the 1979 UK election (there was 7% in the difference) and a Labour Party government had come to power instead. Are we really to suppose that *Duran Duran* would have produced a different kind of music? That certain melodies can only exist in monetarist societies? Of course, there are no parallel universes where we can peer in and compare, but my question can be answered with the common-sense assumption that something as broad and detached as the makeup of a government does not filter all the way down directly to how a band chooses to compose its music. *Duran Duran* would still have sung their songs if James Callaghan had been prime minister and instead they would probably have been seen, by journalists, as a band epitomizing a new 1980s proletarian post-modernism, or whatever. It is never hard to make general sweeping unfalsifiable claims about art and politics (or religion) and to link abstract ideas to random aesthetic phenomena. But it is not unreasonable for us to suppose that art does follow its own internal logic, something that is quite separate to the wider society, and religion, in which it is embedded. The system of art has a *relative autonomy* (to borrow the (modern) Greek philosopher Nicos Poulantzas's phrase). It was other bands and singers, and their own inner creative urges, rather than Tory government, that shaped *Duran Duran*'s output. Let me apply the same skepticism to Zen art. It is true that tea ceremony, haiku, and swordsmanship all existed within the Zen community. That is to say, they were practiced by people who described their world and actions, and arts and practices, through the paradigm of Zen (belief in *non-duality, emptiness,* and *thereness*). But each of these arts, tea ceremony, haiku, and kendo, also existed outside of Zen, that is, were practiced by people not at all affiliated with the Zen religion. And so my question is, were they Zen arts or were they arts sometimes practiced by Zen people? I have argued above that culture and belief are connected. But each has a relative autonomy from the other. Either can change without the other changing accordingly. A society can go from Feudalism to Capitalism and still be writing haiku, as the contrast between Zen Basho and socialist Tsuru Akira shows. Similarly, art can change and beliefs remain the same. The shift from tanka poetry to haiku poetry historically coincided with nothing in particular.

It is true that religions hook themselves on to prevailing cultural norms and expression, and that these start off as historical accidents but become irreplaceable badges of identity later. Christianity, particularly in Western Europe, retains vestiges of Roman Empire times; Shinto shrines are basically renovated ancient rice warehouses; and Buddhist temples are an evolution of Hindu architecture. But it is always a mistake to see these cultural forms as anything more than historical happenstance. For instance, if history had been a bit different and Buddhists had church-like buildings and Christians had temple-like edifices, would the basic doctrines of Buddhism (belief in the Dharma, for instance) and Christianity (monotheism, for example) have been any different. Of course not. In fact, that is why the famous Zen exhortations to "kill the Buddha" (as in, don't get too attached to visual forms) are not actually that radical or unique. Most of the flock of any major religion will have an awareness at some point that their cultural forms and their basic beliefs are not connected and must not be completely confused. But this is not to say that the connection between a religion's cultural forms and art and belief is completely random. As I argued earlier culture, value, and belief are linked. Rather the connection between them is a negative one. Christians could have built temples, but never brothels. There is Zen in the drinking of tea, but not in the downing of straight vodka shots. Art that goes against a religion's beliefs will not survive in the religion. All other art, whatever its form, will otherwise be adopted and *justified* by that religion's beliefs. This is important because if we do not recognize this relative autonomy between art and belief there is a danger that we will draw false analogies between them. The linking of Zen to its arts, such as that done by Suzuki, is a stark example of this danger since it led him into awkward contradiction.

Let us look at some of the ways Suzuki was linking Zen philosophy to Zen culture. Let us start with the laconic nature of haiku poetry. Suzuki, as we have seen, links this to the thusness of Zen, the awareness of here and now in the here and now. However, we have to remember that this "thusness" is not in linear time. As such, the notion that a poem with seven syllables is closer to the non-linear eternal now than a poem with a hundred syllables because the seven-syllable poem is quicker to recite misunderstands the notion of the eternal now. If thusness is beyond time then it is beyond time. Seven is no closer to it than one hundred. Suzuki himself even seems to understand this for a moment ("even seven syllables is too much") before reconnecting with his assumption that laconicity implies thusness.

We see the same with the Zen in the tea ceremony. The presumption here is that the stillness and sparsity of movement make the ceremony more Zen than would be the case with a wild dance party. But there is the danger here that Suzuki is connecting Zen with quietism, that is, the idea that it is the meditative state itself (dhyāna), and not the wisdom or knowledge (prajñā) derived from it that is the satori. As Suzuki explains,

> *Dhyana* is generally translated as 'meditation,' or 'a concentrated state of consciousness,' whereas what Zen proposes is not to make us realize this, but to bring about the awakening of a higher spiritual power so as to come directly in contact with reality itself. This power, called *prajna* in Sanskrit ... is the highest form of intuition we humans are in possession of.[15]

This is a thorny issue as Zen is very much connected to the physical act of meditation, zazen, without which there would be no Zen to speak of. Suzuki comments, confusingly, "Strictly speaking, Zen is no more, no less than our daily life, and there is nothing to teach specifically designated as Zen. But as Zen differentiated itself as such and has a long history behind it, it has developed its own method of training students."[16] This training method is *zazen* (although Suzuki also sees the manual labor monks engage in at their temples to also be part of their training.) But how much do other acts that simulate zazen, such as the tea ceremony, actually become the same as zazen. One thing to note from Suzuki's description of the tea ceremony in his book *Zen in Japanese Culture* is the fact that the practitioner does not enter a meditative state. Rather the Zen quality of the tea ceremony is in the relaxation and quietness rather than the mediation. But this goes against the notion that Zen is to be found in all our actions, quiet or not. There are a series of paintings in Zen called the Ten Oxherding Pictures which show "stages of Zen discipline."[17] As these pictures seem to demonstrate, Zen is to be found in the bustle of the marketplace as much as in the quietness of a tea hut. Bernard Faure argues that Suzuki was never fully able to come to grips with the issue of quietism in Zen.[18] Zen is about meditation, but it is also about everything else you do when not meditating. Ascribing special value to the quietness and calmness of the tea ceremony perhaps compounded the confusion.

Another example of the problem of linking Zen to bits of human life rather than the whole lot is the example of Zen in the art of swordsmanship. Again, the link between swordsmanship and Zen is being made on the grounds that when highly trained swordsmen do their swordsmanship they do so unconsciously, moving naturally as though they were an extension of the sword and the sword was just moving automatically. This creates two issues. Is Zen, then, just about states of unconsciousness? Am I closer to Zen the more automatically I can do something? The second problem, one I raised earlier, is that if you can do swordsmanship and archery in Zen, what else can you do? Motorcycle maintenance, social working, cooking, outer drainpipe lamination? And indeed, as we all know that there have been a plethora of "Zen in the art of whatever" books in recent decades claiming that this is so.[19]

The cynicism of many about this is understandable since Zen is a whole religion and not something to help us to do random manual activities better. But the problem seems to be that in describing Zen as simply life itself, Suzuki had thrown away those cultural forms that identify Zen and make it the living religion that it is. It was he who had created the monster of Zen popularization.[20]

Zen and "Zen"

The problem with linking Zen philosophy to Zen culture and assuming that one reflects the other is that one is, intentionally or otherwise, committing the fallacy of "equivocation," that is, taking advantage of the ambiguities in the word "Zen" to make claims about Zen that are not rationally possible. "Zen is the mountain" (as Suzuki exclaimed in *An Introduction to Zen Buddhism*) and Zen is a state of mind when practicing swordsmanship. These two statements can only make sense and can be put together when we realize that the word "Zen" has different distinct meanings. There is "Zen" that is a specific cultural form that we can see in haiku poetry and swordsmanship. It represents and promotes the values of quietism, laconicity, the pursuit of unconscious awareness in the practice of certain arts and crafts. And then there is "Zen" which is the philosophy of prajñā, the belief that knowledge is not ultimately dependent on the split between knower and known because behind the dichotomy of knower and known there is the True Person of No Rank, that is, you that is just there in the here and now, regardless of what else is going on. It is easy to see how "Zen" the art form can be used as a metaphor or symbol of Zen philosophy. After all, the True Person of No Rank is just there not moving or consciously thinking, hence the connection with the stillness and automaticity of the tea-ceremony, swordsmanship, and haiku composing. But this is a mistake.

The True Person of No Rank is beyond space and time. He/she/it is just there whether everything else moves fast or slow, or if everything else is organized or in confusion, or if everything else is complicated or simple. In other words, Zen is again making a clear distinction between the world of everyday phenomena, which includes your own conscious acting self, and that deeper self and knowledge which stands detached and watching, which can never be part of this world of form, including the world of time. As Suzuki comments: "What we truly and really have is the one spiritual world, that is, the One, undiscriminated, indeterminate, undistinguished, undifferentiated."[21] However, this spiritual world, detached as it is from form is not sustainable as it is purely nothing without form. Suzuki states further.

> But our human consciousness is so designed that it cannot remain in this state of oneness, of sameness; and we somehow begin to reflect upon it in order to become conscious of it, to give it a clear definition to make it the subject of contemplation, and also to break it up into pieces so that the energy eternally sealed up in silence and inactivity will become vocal and manifest itself in the dynamics of human activities.[22]

The One, a nothingness, breaks up into the many, the world of forms in which we do things, and in which our cultural forms dwell. However, Suzuki makes the further important point that the connection between Oneness and the many is not about things breaking up and being put back together again. One and many, while a numerical metaphor, is not about counting the things in the world. The One is beyond time and beyond counting. It does not exist in the same series as the many. As Suzuki says: "But we must not imagine that the breaking up of the One into the Many is a development in time-process." In other words, the One never goes away even when we go away from it. It is always just there, no matter how busy or loud or consciously distracted or un-Zen-like in our behavior we are. As Suzuki says:

> ... we have to remember that the world of spirit is right here, we are right in it, we have never departed from it. Even when we seem to be the

abject slaves of the Many and the playthings of dualistic ratiocination, the world of spirit is encircling us, is circulating through us, has its axis of movement in our workaday life.[23]

All this makes for a very complicated connection between the One and the many (it is there even when it is not there) that is encapsulated somewhat in the pithy declaration from the Heart Sutra: "Emptiness is form, form is emptiness." In other words, the formless Oneness, the True Person of No Rank, is precisely there where there is form and where there is rank. It cannot be ever otherwise.

> Where there is no form there is not emptiness (*sunyata*). For emptiness is formlessness and has not selfhood, no individuality, and therefore it is always with form. Form is emptiness and emptiness is form. If emptiness were something limited, something resisting, something impure in the sense of allowing something else to get mixed with it, it would never be with form, in form, and form itself.[24]

Taking into consideration this inseparable connection between form and emptiness, we can acknowledge that the conflation of Zen as a philosophy and Zen as a cultural form is not a confusion but actually the world in operation precisely as Zen predicts it to be. We cannot avoid truth, even at its most universal and pure to the extent that it is empty, becoming attached to form. And yet Zen will go one step further and say that what is unavoidable is also to be avoided. We must never confuse the forms in the world, the many, with the emptiness, the One. The fact that we always do confuse form and the many with emptiness and the one is the clearest demonstration we have that they are never the same. To quote Rinzai again: "Here in this lump of red flesh there is a True Man of no rank."[25]

In other words, our experience of the world as conscious beings is that it is infested with a contradiction that never goes away. We are here and now but that here and now-ness can never be part of the world over there, the world of forms we also see. We are here and we are there, at the same time, even though both are separate. How can this be? As we have seen, materialists nowadays often try to solve this by reducing our "hereness" to an element of over thereness, as in, for example, neurological phenomena, or whatever. Some materialists will even go so far as to eliminate the issue of "hereness" all together. This is the school of mind philosophy known as the eliminationists.[26] This is necessary, they will argue, if we are to continue to have a rational description of our world. However, as Suzuki cautions.

> Irrationality is also a form of reasoning. We cannot escape it. The danger arises when experience is denied in order to put reason foremost, while the fact of life tells us that the latter grows from the former and not *vice versa*. Reasoning must conform to life, and when there is something in life which refuses to be dealt with by reason, it is the latter and not the former that has to make a new start.[27]

What this clash between Zen as a culture and Zen as a philosophy reveals is that "truth," that universal description of reality to be applicable everywhere in the abstract, only ever presents itself to us in a particular cultural form. It is paradox but the solution is to accept it: "In truth, the Buddhist solution of the great problem of life consists in not solving it at all, and they contend that the not-solving is really the solving."[28] However, there is a great danger here in the assumption that the great problems of life just solve themselves. This brings us to the thorny issue of Zen ethics.

Zen Ethics

The point about Zen is that it takes life as it is. Its philosophy is based on emptiness which will always be one with form, which means that really any form, so long as it be the form that we find as we live and move in this world, can be that of Zen. In his book *Living by Zen* (1950), Suzuki makes a distinction between "living Zen" and "living by Zen." Living Zen is just simply reality and all that is in it as it is. "We all live Zen, non-sentient as well as sentient ...." But whereas animals live Zen, it is humans, on account of their consciousness who not only live Zen but can live *by* Zen: "It is man alone that can live by Zen as well as live Zen. To live Zen is not enough; we must live by it, which means that we must have the consciousness of living it, although this consciousness is beyond what we generally understand by it."[29] How should humans live by Zen? What is the good and moral Zen life? For Suzuki this is the wrong question to ask since Zen is beyond morality. Morality is about dualistic thinking, a subject looking out on the world of objects and evaluating and judging them. Zen, we must remember, believes such subject-object distinctions to be relative and not absolute forms of knowledge. Hence any judgments we make, including moral judgments, on the basis of our dualistic frame of mind are ultimately false, or rather not as absolutely true as they could be if made from the standpoint of Zen where subject and object just come and go. The point is that moral judgment involves fantasizing about another world that is not actually there. We are talking about "should" and "must," but not about "is." Zen implies the radical consciousness of here and now as here and now. To go beyond this is to enter falsehood and partiality. For Zen, morality implies vagueness and judgment about over there instead of the clear vision and decisiveness of here and now. As Suzuki explains:

> The living by Zen is more than being merely moral. Morality restrains, binds; Zen releases and brings us out into a wider and freer realm of life. Morality is not creative, and exhausts itself by trying to be other than itself, or rather trying to be itself. The living by Zen means to remain itself, to be complete by itself, and therefore it is always self-working; it gives out what it has, and never tries or contrives to be other than itself. With Zen every morning is a good morning, every day a fine day, no matter how stormy. Morality always binds itself with the ideas of good and evil, just and unjust, virtuous and unvirtuous, and cannot go beyond them; for if it goes, it will no longer be itself; it is its own nature that it cannot be free and self-independent. Zen is, however, not tied up with any such ideas; it is as free as the bird flying, the fish swimming, and the lilies blooming.[30]

In this sense Zen espouses a very radical and absolute form of what is called in philosophy *virtue ethics*, the view that morality is ensured not through rules or rational judgment but through an instinctive or cultivated awareness of how to behave appropriately at any moment.[31] The claim here seems to be that the wisdom of Zen is such that the fully enlightened will behave, without a moment's thought or hesitation, in a manner that is in-keeping with the natural ways of the world. The cultivation of such virtue ethics, it seems, comes from trying to regain the naturalness that humans are endowed with when they are not in a dualistic frame of mind. Suzuki makes a distinction between nature and human consciousness which has become divided from nature. For Suzuki, nature has an innate moral goodness to it and the more we can become one with nature, that is, behave in a natural unintended way, the more appropriate our behavior is. Suzuki comments:

> It is Man who accommodates himself to meet Nature. Nature's "must" is absolute. Man must accept it. In this respect Nature has something of the divine will. This is the reason, I think, why being natural or spontaneous has a certain alluring quality in it. When a child performs deeds which polite society would condemn as undignified or improper or sometimes even immoral, the offenses are not only condoned but accepted as acts of innocent charming childlikeness. There is something divine in being spontaneous and being not at all hampered by human conventionalities and their artificial sophisticated hypocrisies. There is something direct and fresh in this not being restrained by anything human, which suggests a divine freedom and creativity. Nature never deliberates, it acts directly out of its own heart, whatever this may mean. Nature is divine in this respect. Its "irrationality" transcends human doubts or ambiguities or equivocations. In our submitting to it or rather accepting it we also transcend ourselves.[32]

The idea seems to be that good and evil is a matter of how near or distant one is from the wider natural flow of the universe. The further one is splitting away from the underlying prajñā consciousness, that non-dualistic seeing what is as it is in the here and now, the more one is entering into evils, those disorders of the spirit that arise when subject and object emerge and one dominates the other. Good and evil are not choices but states of mind. When one is fully in tune with the prajñā consciousness one is no more capable of doing evil than a flower growing on a tree or a fish swimming in a lake. You are just there, moving, and so is everything else. Nothing is different, nothing opposed, nothing resisting. This is when one is virtuous, good, and ethical. When subject and object are transcended, body and mind have dropped away, and all is not just as it should be but as it is. It is the beautiful dream of Man before the Fall when all our actions were simply and naturally good. It is about being one with nature and submitting to the codependent arising of our planet's ecosystem and shunning the evil selfishness of human egotistical rationality that has alienated us from nature.

Zen Way of Life

What is it like, then, this Zen way of life? The ideal of Zen is that one reaches a state of inner certitude such that one returns to the spontaneity and innocence of nature. Zen is about life as it is. This does not mean a retreat from social engagement, since life includes this as well. As mentioned elsewhere, the Ten Ox-Herding Pictures, that series of pictures from medieval Japan drawn to illustrate the Zen path to enlightenment express worldliness. As Suzuki explains:

> In "The Ten Cow-herding Pictures" the last scene shows a happy-looking man entering the market place. The market place contrasts with the mountain retreat: the former is the place where a man serves society, while the latter is where he trains himself to be qualified for public work. The monastery is not meant just to be a hiding place from the worries of the world; on the contrary, it is a training station where a man equips himself for life's battlefield, that is, to do all that can possibly be done for his community.[33]

In other words, Zen does not set up any dualism between the world of Zen and the world of ordinary non-Zen. If you live life by Zen this should not change you and make you behave differently as though you had joined a particular cult or ideology. As Suzuki says, " ... Zen is not to be identified with any particular brand of 'ism.'"[34] This is because, to repeat the point, Zen is life, and as such it excludes nothing that is not part of life, including our daily morals and activities. As Suzuki says, "In fact, Zen, being life itself, contains everything that goes into the make-up of life: Zen is poetry, Zen is philosophy, Zen is morality. Wherever there is life-activity, there is Zen."[35] The point is that Zen, the knowledge of the here and now is utterly affirming. While it cannot be linked to any "-ism," it can be compatible with any of them. As Suzuki also wrote:

> Zen has no special doctrine of philosophy, no set of concepts or intellectual formulas, except that it tries to release one from the bondage of birth and death, by means of certain intuitive modes of understanding peculiar to itself. It is, therefore, extremely flexible in adapting itself to almost any philosophy and moral doctrine as long as its intuitive teaching is not interfered with. It may be found wedded to anarchism or fascism, communism or democracy, atheism or idealism, or any political or economic dogmatism.[36]

Now, do not be shocked by his reference to "fascism," just focus on the consistency in what he is saying. Zen offers a level of knowledge that is simply beyond any particular ideology. Zen is working from the field of emptiness where stands the True Person of No Rank. Ideologies are, by contrast, relative and partial belief systems that organize the world through principles and abstractions. They are not about life as it is directly lived and experienced but about how life ought to be in an idealized world never to be directly known.

But does this mean that the people of Zen have no opinion about the world, or rather have any opinion they just happen to feel "intuitively" about the world. Are they the ultimate nihilists, just cruising through life following their random intuitions and instincts believing in nothing but just going with the flow? At the Mexico conference on *Zen and Psychoanalysis* Suzuki had various questions submitted to him, such as "What is Zen's attitude toward ethics? Toward political and economic deprivation? Toward the individual's position and responsibility toward his society?" He dismissed such questions saying, " … as I went over them I discovered that most of them seemed to miss the central or pivotal point around which Zen moves."[37] But he did then give a lengthy roundabout response in which he seemed to make the argument that Zen is ethical because we have sayings from Zen masters that seem ethical. For instance, the usually boorish Master Jōshū (Zhaozhou in Chinese) once kindly offered to go to hell ahead of everyone else because "without my first going to hell, who would be waiting there to save people like you?"[38] Indeed, I have in my time met many Zen practitioners. Almost all of them are friendly, good humored and down to earth, some of them are slightly over-intense types, and very occasionally you do get the odd sanctimonious more-satoried-than-thou sort (as you do in any religion). But on the whole, they are a nice bunch of people. However, the assertion that a religion is ethical because the people who practice it behave ethically is philosophically questionable. What are the grounds Zen gives for us to act nice to each other?

Looking at Suzuki's own life, he certainly had a sense of ethics and was engaged in the issues of the day, often penning newspaper articles and essays laced with judgments and opinions.[39] He was not at all impressed, for example, with the whole Beatnik fad in America even though it revered him and hailed Zen as a justification for its non-conformist ways. Mihoko Okamura, his assistant in later years, recounts how Suzuki never wasted paper. She writes, "It was a private protest against the wanton waste of the modern world, especially the irresponsible destruction of our forests. I often heard him voice his protest in this regard, as well as his warning that humans would pay dearly for their senseless ways."[40] Such environmentalist sentiments are noble and to be admired. But they do also demonstrate that, with all Suzuki's protests to the contrary, he did have an ideology, in this case a belief in environmentalism. Now, it may be argued that Suzuki was merely making the point that humans do exist within nature and that this is not about ideology but about everyday life which comes from nature and is at one with nature. We saw earlier how important nature was for Suzuki and how it grew out of the Zen intuition that we are all connected to the world and all within it. Human behavior is just as much a part of nature as the flight of birds in autumn or the blooming of flowers in spring. Environmentalism is merely minimal awareness of the natural state humans are in and need to stay in. But environmentalism is an ideology, a political platform, and an economic dogma. It works, first of all, from the assumption that certain human behaviors are closer to nature than others. For example, irrigating a field is assumed to be more natural than building a cement factory. But why should this be? Farming is not a natural activity for humans and the transition from hunter-gatherer lifestyles to agriculture in history was an enormous ecological transformation—not at all part of the cycle of nature. Furthermore, an exclusive focus on our ecosystems is also an ideological decision to shift attention from human history as the history of class struggle to human history as a minor and irrelevant event in the wider bio-chemical totality. (And, by the way, while we are on the subject, that last Ox-Herding picture showing the return to the marketplace demonstrates pro-mercantile capitalist tendencies.[41]) Now, you may agree with environmentalism, I certainly do, but to claim it is not an ideology is the ultimate ideological blindness.

Suzuki's view of nature, as a realm of innate goodness, is a highly romanticized one. Such an image of nature is easy when all we see is that which is pleasant in nature. When we visualize nature the way the haiku poets of Zen do—flowers growing, frogs jumping, cicada chirping—we can see why conformity to its rhythms and patterns is something good, pure, and to be praised. But nature is also nasty and brutal. Let us imagine those other parts of creation where for countless years, even before the Ascent of Man, for example, animals have killed each other viciously. Think of baby turtles which have since times remote been gorged by birds before they can trundle their way to the ocean. Or think of those parasites that eat away slowly and painfully the innards of other animals. This too is nature. It is a cruel, ruthless world where destruction is merciless and as unstoppable as a mucky landslide rumbling and tumbling its way to a sleeping village. Animals kill one another driven by a remorseless instinct with no more moral self-reflection than if they were scratching an itch. In nature, cruelty is automatic and unrelenting.

No Mind or Mindless

The problem with Suzuki's naturalist morality, the assumption that a return to the spontaneity and pure simplicity of nature is good, is manifest most starkly, and I am sorry to return to this point but it cannot be avoided, in his writings about the samurai and their swords. It seems that in Suzuki's view, once you have emptied your mind and become one with the world, moral judgments are an irrelevancy. Things just happen. Rain falls. Frogs jump. Swords slice. Here is one of Suzuki's more shocking descriptions of the "art" of swordsmanship:

> The sword is generally associated with killing, and most of us wonder how it can come into connection with Zen, which is a school of Buddhism teaching the gospel of love and mercy. The fact is that the art of swordsmanship distinguishes between the sword that kills and the sword that gives life. The one that is used by a technician cannot go any further than killing, for he never appeals to the sword unless he intends to kill. The case is altogether different with one who is compelled to lift the sword. For it is really not he but the sword itself that does the killing. He has no desire to do harm to anybody, but the enemy appears and makes himself a victim. It is as though the sword performs automatically its function of justice, which is the function of mercy.[42]

The problem with this passage is that so much of what he is saying here is completely compatible with the naturalist Zen morality Suzuki has outlined in his descriptions of living by Zen. If one has transcended the subject and object divide, has become one with the world, is devoid of desire or intentionality, and swings a sword and deprives another of life, where is the immorality in this? It is just life as it is lived. It is a return to a greater spiritual oneness where everything, including weapons, perform automatically, and once this automaticity is maintained justice and mercy has been fulfilled. As Slavoj Žižek comments,

> ... does not this description of killing present the ultimate case of the phenomenological attitude which, instead of intervening in reality,

just lets things appear the way they are? It is the sword itself which does the killing; it is the enemy himself who just appears and makes himself a victim—I am not responsible; I am reduced to a passive observer of my own acts.[43]

There is no getting around the fact that Suzuki walked himself into this amoral position. Of course, it is reasonable to assume that in writing this Suzuki was merely being loyal to the Zen culture in all its forms to which he was committed and which he had taken upon himself to present to the world. Like a good propagandist, he took Zen as it is, warts and all, and rather than try and hide its past collaboration with Bushido, sought to find justifications for it. Suzuki had argued that Zen could do no wrong (Zen is life itself) and he was going to bravely stick to this argument. I have already stated my belief that Suzuki was not a warmonger or lover of violence and I do think he never meant his words about swordsmanship to be anything other than abstract romanticizing. But still we have a problem. Suzuki, unlike Okakura, was unable to see any difference between drinking tea and killing people. This is a moral failure no matter how we try to frame it. Why did it happen?

Part Animal

The problem goes back to Suzuki's views on the relationship between humans and nature. As stated, Suzuki believed that humans were different to animals because they had a certain self-awareness. However, he also seemed to believe that this was a weakness in humans and that animals, because they do things unaware with an instinctive automaticity, are the morally superior sentient beings. Humans have a tendency to think too much. This puts them outside of the cycle of nature. It makes them interfere with those cycles and to create obstacles and artifices that block the natural flow of the cosmos. Whereas the cycle of nature is constantly self-corrective, moving forward as it is meant to do, leaving nothing remaining, inscribing no traces of its deliberations, humans make and do that which sticks out, smears marks on the cosmos, marks which remain as blemishes in the purity of nature that should be just as it is, without trace. The ideal human is the one who can just move without leaving anything behind. Like the amoral samurai, it does what it does and moves on. But the point is that humans have the remarkable ability to be aware of their own instincts, to know that they have some control over them, and to be able to ask if following their instinct is the morally right thing to do. No other animal, it seems, does this. The result is that humans have broken the cycle of nature they have evolved into and have created history. But history is *contingent*, meaning that every moment of history could turn out differently. By contrast the great cycles of nature can be pictured as mechanical and fixed. Think, for example, of the knowledge astronomers have of the future events, for instance the fact that Earth will transit Mars on May 16, 2552. There is no narrative in nature, just episodes that repeat. History, on the other hand, is a narrative. It moves forward through time with no episode ever being repeated exactly the same. Each moment, each year, each epoch produces patterns of human culture that always seem to be different in some respect. Think of the evolution of movies. How did movies in the 1990s get to be so different to those of the 1950s? There is no obvious one explanation for this, it was the product of a myriad of small changes through time made by each generation and the movie makers they spawned. But note that no other animal is capable of such cultural inventiveness.

As I have said, humans have a strange gift that no other animal has: they know what they are doing and can act on that knowledge. It is this ability that makes humans the moral beings that they are. Humans are condemned to always have moral choices in their actions. Not just that, but by making these moral choices, humans are also condemned to live in a constantly changing world, changing due to their own moral choices. We decide to behave differently in the world and the world then becomes different, burdening us with further decisions. The curse of human freedom and history. For instance, on the issue of cooking and its variation across time and culture, Suzuki had this to say.

> Be that as it may, humans will with raw ingredients, grill them, simmer them, boil them, steam them, roast them, dry them, pickle them, or

cook them with various other methods. Such are humans. And so with a fraction of ingredients being made into plenty, humans eat in abundance. Needless to say it is the principle of "dumplings before flowers [花より団子]" but there is also "flowers before dumplings [団子より花]. Humans are a nuisance, but they are also fascinating. Humans, being human, never know where to start or stop. This is the development of culture.⁴⁴

The point is, then, that Suzuki's naturalist morality, his call for us to return to the primordial instinctive morality that those beings still in the cycle of nature experience, involves a denial of the human experience of history, the fact that all our actions have emerged in a wider context which gives them meaning and consequence. To say, as Suzuki said, of a samurai that "For it is really not he but the sword itself that does the killing" displays outrageous naivety about human history. All swords since the mists of time have been swung for some reason or other. There is a history to everything we do.

A Bit of History

The official history of Zen is a simple one. It starts off, as Suzuki describes it, in the following way.

> Traditionally Zen is considered to have been transmitted by the Buddha to his foremost disciple, Mahākāśyapa, when the Buddha held out a bunch of flowers to his congregation, the meaning of which was at once grasped by Mahākāśyapa, who quietly smiled at him.⁴⁵

This was the first special transmission of Zen, a transmission that continued down through history via further patriarchs in India, and subsequently in China after the patriarch Bodhidharma come over from India, and on it has passed right up to today. It is a transmission that is based on intergenerational and interpersonal connection, and hence has a *genealogy*, a lineage of patriarchs and roshi throughout history passing on Zen from India to China and on to Japan. Of course, commenting on the Mahākāśyapa story, Suzuki acknowledges that "The historicity of this incident is justly criticized, but knowing the value of Enlightenment we cannot ascribe the authority of Zen just to such an episode as this. Zen was in fact handed over not only to Mahākāśyapa but to all beings who will follow the steps of the Buddha, the Enlightened One."[46] Suzuki was willing to allow for fabrication and myth, but only up to a point. The history of Zen is still a smooth and continuous passage through time. There are pivotal moments in its development and key patriarchs created certain concepts to add further voltage to the transmission. For instance, according to Suzuki, Bodhidharma emphasized the concept of "way," Eno brought focus on "mind," and Rinzai introduced the central notion of the True Person of No Rank.[47]

Furthermore, the evolution of Zen is also tied, by Suzuki, to innate cultural differences between India, China, and Japan. Zen emerged in India but was not fully appreciated there since the Indians are too abstract and metaphysical in their thinking. When dealing with concrete issues, the Indian mind tends toward mythological exaggerations. Zen fared better in China where the Chinese mind is a down to earth practical one, closer to the here and now that Zen deals with. But even the Chinese mind was not enough. It is only when Zen hits Japan that it can reach its full fruition. Japan was the Goldilocks zone for full Zen maturation, lying as it does within the not too abstract and not too concrete range. Suzuki made this claim most forcefully in *Japanese Spirituality* (1944). The book is mostly about Jodo Shinshu, a different branch of Buddhism, but for Suzuki, all Japanese Buddhism, including Zen, is part of the same mindset, or rather *reisei* (spirituality). This Japanese spirituality is not the same as Buddhism, but it proved the perfect platform for its uploading. To explain the difference of this "spirituality" specific to Japan and Buddhism in general, Suzuki harnesses botanical metaphors to demonstrate that while Buddhism and Japanese spirituality were different there was a symbiotic relationship between them:

> Still were it not for Buddhism I imagine we should have nothing much to say about Japanese spirituality. Yet to call it a Japanized Buddhism would be to confuse cause and effect, like saying that because grass

will not grow without rain, therefore rain is grass. The growth of plants and trees is brought about thanks to rain, sun, wind, and soil, but they do not themselves produce plants and trees. They have their own primary essence. I should like to take up Japanese spirituality as one such primary essence.[48]

This Japanese spirituality, which Suzuki characterizes as a connectedness to the earth, as in soil and ground, has motored the changes in Japan's modes of production throughout its history. For instance, the shift between rule by the aristocracy in the Heian period to the (Zen loving) warrior classes was due to this earth connectedness thing rather than the usual socio-political and economic factors more conventional historians would tend to cite.

> It was inevitable that Heian culture would be superseded by a culture coming from the earth. Those representing this culture, with a foothold in the country, were the samurai, who had immediate connections to the peasantry. Therefore the nobility was finally to surrender before the gates of the samurai. This did not happen because of the samurai's physical strength, but because their roots were deep in the earth. Historians may call this economic or material strength (or physical force), but to me it is the spirit of the earth.[49]

And as touched upon, it was this earthly spirituality which made Japanese Buddhism different to what it had been in India and China. The Chinese had been just too practical and the Indians just too abstract for a fully matured Buddhism.

> Chinese Buddhism was incapable of passing beyond cause and effect; Indian Buddhism sunk into the depths of emptiness. Japanese spirituality alone, in not destroying cause and effect, nor the existence of this world, succeeded in including all things as they are completely within Amida's Light. This was possible with Japanese spirituality alone, and it was the Kamakura period that produced the opportunity for it.[50]

The point is that Buddhism emerges in Japan as it does according to a consciousness that is more like a force of nature, something smooth, unstoppable, with the sense that it was always meant to happen as it did. There are none of the usual vulgar social and economic vagaries and vicissitudes that are commonly seen to shape a religion in its growth through history. All along there was a spiritual DNA in the Japanese people that was just going to grow things the way it did. Going back to Zen specifically, Suzuki does allow for the fact that Zen piggy-backs on other religions and philosophies as it moves through the world and history. But these particular colorings are merely vehicles for the transmission of Zen, to be discarded when no longer needed. Zen is always pure and detached from whatever forms it has had to hide in. In *Zen and Japanese Culture*, he writes:

> Theoretically speaking, Zen has nothing to do with nationalism. As long as it is a religion, its mission has universal validity, and its field of applicability is not limited to any one nationality. But from the point of view of history it is subject to accidents and particularization. When Zen first came to Japan, it became identified with persons steeped in Confucianism and patriotic spirit, and Zen naturally took their color unto itself; that is to say, Zen was not received in Japan in its pure form, free of the effect of all accidents of place and time. Not only that, the Japanese followers themselves were willing to take Zen with everything that came with it, until later accidentals were separated from the body to which they were attached and came to establish themselves independently, even in defiance of their original association.[51]

The arguments and analogies Suzuki uses (rain and plants, bodies, and accidentals) are clever because they reflect a notion of history that is evolutionary in a way that allows for accidental events but still emphasizes how these accidents do not shape Zen, rather they merely allow for it to be as it is. Zen will always from beginning to end remain pure and ahistorical.

Zen and the Problem of History

But let us pose the question here: would Zen have ever happened if the ancient Zen masters Hui-neng (Eno in Japanese) or Lin-chi (Rinzai in Japanese) had never been born? This is not a koan or a mondo. I ask because it reveals a quandary that Suzuki faces. Is Zen something absolute, like the constants of physics that just have to be the way they are, or is it something contingent, something that may never have emerged in human history had random events been a bit different? Let us remind ourselves, for a moment, of how Suzuki defines and describes Zen. This is from his influential book *An Introduction to Zen Buddhism*:

> Some say that as Zen is admittedly a form of mysticism it cannot claim to be unique in the history of religion. Perhaps so; but Zen is a mysticism of its own order. It is mystical in the sense that the sun shines, that the flower blooms, that I hear at this moment somebody beating a drum in the street. If these are mystical facts, Zen is brim-full of them. When a Zen master was once asked what Zen was, he replied, "Your everyday thought." Is this not plain and most straightforward? It has nothing to do with any sectarian spirit. Christians as well as Buddhists can practise Zen just as big fish and small fish are both contentedly living in the same ocean. Zen is the ocean, Zen is the air, Zen is the mountain, Zen is thunder and lightning, the spring flower, summer heat, and winter snow; nay, more than that, Zen is the man. With all the formalities, conventionalisms, and superadditions that Zen has accumulated in its long history, its central fact is very much alive. The special merit of Zen lies in this: that we are still able to see into this ultimate fact without being biased by anything.[52]

"Zen is the mountain." But mountains are not part of history, they are part of nature, and their description is one of geology, something devoid of human will. Let us consider the difference between geology and history. In Japan there are many small mounds made from piled up rocks, called *kofun*, that were built by ancient (roughly fourth–sixth century) people. They dot the landscape and many people, myself included, like to go and stare at them, these lithic monuments to a distant past. But why will I gaze at a *kofun* and not at any other mound or pile of rocks that may be right beside it or close by? Because when I look at a *kofun* I perceive the traces of other humans. I am reading their story. The random pile of rocks beside the *kofun* is part of a geology which is not a story but a mechanical explanation of nature. In other words, nature is simply there: ocean, air, mountains, and spring flowers are as they are. They offer no traces. But history is those bits of nature upon which humans tramped, leaving their marks from which we can tell their story. This is why the world is not equal for humans. A *kofun* will always have more value for us than a natural pile of rocks. In saying that Zen is the mountain, Suzuki seems to be pushing Zen away from any particular story and allowing Zen to stand just there as it is. Furthermore, he declares "Zen is the man." This is not meant to mean people as in homo sapiens, but people as in the possessors of that transcendental consciousness that is never just one more object in the world. If Zen is linked to this then Zen cannot ever be part of history because it is the very site from which history is seen and experienced. It cannot enter into it, just as an eye cannot see itself. And so, from this perspective, we can say yes. If Hui-neng or Lin-chi had never been born Zen would still have happened. But if Zen is so independent of history why do we even bother using the word "Zen." Why not use the words "life" or "reality" or "mind"? What is this "Zen" we do talk about, this "Zen" we could just as easily not talk about and the world would be the same as it always is. Or, is there something wrong with what I am saying? Is Zen, in fact, not something that is just there but actually something that had to be developed by human society, something with its own contingent history that has allowed us to use the word "Zen" as we do? Is "Zen" just there or does it have a starting point and path in history, this is the question.

Zen Duels

The Chinese philosopher Hu Shih (1891–1962) believed that Zen did have a starting date, or rather starting period, and this was Song Dynasty China. But to make this point he felt obliged to force a showdown with Suzuki in an article published in 1953 in the journal *Philosophy East and West* entitled "Ch'an (Zen) Buddhism in China: Its history and method" in which he took aim and fired shots at Suzuki's ahistorical approach. Hu Shih stomped into Zen saloon all-ahollering, guns ablaze, before Suzuki even had time to draw. He hit Suzuki with this stinger: " ... I have never concealed from [Suzuki] my disappointment in his method of approach. My greatest disappointment has been that, according to Suzuki and his disciples, Zen is illogical, irrational, and, therefore, beyond our intellectual understanding."[53] He continued his volley, mouthing Suzuki's own words back at him.

> It is this denial of the capability of the human intelligence to understand and evaluate Zen that I emphatically refuse to accept. Is the so-called Ch'an or Zen really so illogical and irrational that it is "altogether beyond the ken of human understanding" and that our rational or rationalistic way of thinking is of no use "in evaluating the truth and untruth of Zen"?[54]

Them's fighting words alright. It is only after this feisty intro that Hu Shih actually gets to the topic of his essay, which is to present his evidence that true Zen history begins in Song China, and not earlier, something that Suzuki had never particularly disputed one way or another before. The assault does seem an intemperate gratuitous trigger-happy one, although I must admit as someone who has been active in Zen scholarship, that I have a sneaking admiration for Hu Shih's style. Too often intellectual talk about Zen is gunned down immediately by gunk about Zen having no philosophy or history or whatever. Maybe Hu Shih was wise to fire first.

Suzuki wrote a rejoinder to Hu Shih's criticism, published in the same journal.[55] Like any debate fought through long text posts, it is not always clear what exactly they are arguing about. They often picked up on non-essential points or unimportant word choices the other made. But it is not hard to see how Hu Shih's vision of Zen history clashes with that of Suzuki's. Suzuki always saw Zen as the product of a direct lineage back to the Buddha. Even if the stories and fables were fictions, the fact of there having been a lineage in some shape or form was never fully doubted. As I have said, various Zen masters did add to Zen, in the sense that they supplied new concepts and understandings, but these were simply further explanations of something that was always there and unchanged. On the other hand, for Hu Shih the intervention of the masters, and more importantly, their disciples (who often remastered their masters) was what created Zen. Hu Shih saw the famous story of Hui-neng, a kitchen boy who secretly attains appointment as the Sixth Patriarch in the face of opposition from the baddie establishment, to be an invention. This was anathema to Suzuki who little doubted the episode. As an aside, it is worth mentioning that Hu Shih's view of Zen history—retro-fabrications of tales about earlier masters by later schools—is actually the scholarly opinion these days, although his particular emphasis on Song China has been questioned.[56]

Furthermore, Hu Shih also has a more complicated view of Asian ethnic diversity than Suzuki (not that that was particularly hard). He points out, for example, that Hui-neng was from a non-Han background. Suzuki, on the other hand, always had a delightfully uncomplicated view of the world's nations and peoples which were divided, for Suzuki, into four great nations: India, where everyone thinks in grand and abstract ways; China, where everyone is so practical; the West (which is one country, effectively), where everyone is a neurotic hyper-rational dualist; and Japan, where everyone has that earthly connectedness spirituality. I am not sure if any other countries other than these four ever actually existed for him. Hu Shih's geography was far more intricate than Suzuki's four-piece jigsaw.

Another major fault line between them, maybe the big one, was the idea that the philosophy of Zen itself could in any way be subject to socio-political factors. For Suzuki, Zen may shape itself to fit a society but no society shapes Zen. Zen is just Zen. For Hu Shih this was not the case. Who got to be patriarch, which lineage survived, and other such matters in Zen history were very much the product of political interference, conditions, and events. Even the most core ideas and practices of Zen could be fashioned specifically to please the crowd. The mere idea of this, economic factors in Zen formation, was unthinkable for Suzuki. He writes,

> Hu Shih is no doubt a brilliant writer and an astute thinker, but his logic of deducing the Zen methodology of irrationalism and "seeming craziness" out of the economic necessity of getting support from the

powerful patrons is, to say the least, illogical and does not add to his rationalistic historicism.[57]

There was never any racket going on in the history of Zen. It was always just Zen, pure and simple. And Zen koans were always spontaneous affairs, and not scripted audience-pleasing performances.

Dercad dhyāna and sitcháin samādhi

Let us go back to my earlier question whether there would be Zen if history had been different. The word "Zen" comes from the Sanskrit word "dhyāna" which means roughly to meditate or, in some usages, to still the mind. As an action—just sitting and stilling the mind— it is undoubtedly common to many, if not all cultures. For instance, according to Celtic scholar, Peter Berresford Ellis, Old Irish had the concept of "dercad," which, according to Ellis, is "an act of meditation, by which Irish mystics would attempt to achieve a state of *sitcháin* or peace."[58] This sounds very much like dhyāna. I first learned about the concept of sitcháin from Ellis's Sister Fidelma mysteries, a series of detective novels he has written under the name of Peter Tremayne set in seventh-century Ireland. The hero of the novel is Sister Fidelma, a sharp minded sleuthing religieuse who occasionally practices dercad to reach sitcháin. Sister Fidelma and Hui-neng lived at the same time as each other. Now, of course, Fidelma is a fictional character created by Peter Berresford Ellis, and Hui-neng is a semi-fictional character created by Song period Shen Hui (if we are to believe Hu Shih). But let us take advantage of this fictionality and imagine in our heads Sister Fidelma and Hui-neng meeting up somewhere along the Silk Road in the seventh century. They would be speaking in Sodgian (not Irish or Chinese or Latin) and Hui-neng would probably say, "I understand dercad, it is the same as the dhyāna of Zen." And Fidelma would say, "And I understand dhyāna, it is the same as dercad in Celtic Christianity." They will equate dhyāna and dercad in this way. But given that Zen's ahistoricity is based on the ahistorical nature of the act and experience of dhyāna, can we then make the same claim for Celtic Christianity, that it too is ahistorical since it knows and practices dercad? Remember, in equating dhyāna and dercad I am mirroring the spirit of Suzuki and the claims he makes for Zen: "It has nothing to do with any sectarian spirit. Christians as well as Buddhists can practice Zen just as big fish and small fish are both contentedly living in the same ocean. Zen is the ocean ... "[59] (note that Zen is not the fish). And many from non-Buddhist faiths have been inspired by Suzuki to make and explore similar claims.[60] So yet again we can state that there would still be Zen even without its history. It would simply be called something else, like "dercad" or "sitcháin," for example. But the problem is, obviously, that Zen cannot be identified exactly with Celtic Christianity because Zen also has its sutras, its patriarchs, its koans, its mondos, and, dare we suggest, its beliefs, for example in a Dharma rather than a "Christian" God. Suzuki did stand his ground when confronting Hu Shih, telling him that specific definable historical beliefs do not describe Zen. However, elsewhere, for example in his 1957 book *Mysticism: Christian and Buddhist* he is quite explicit in seeing Zen Buddhism as something distinct from Christianity in terms of its symbols, history, and beliefs. For instance, he says, "whenever I see a crucified figure of Christ, I cannot help thinking of the gap that lies deep between Christianity and Buddhism. This gap is symbolic of the psychological division separating the East from the West."[61]

Indeed, going back to Suzuki's defensive tirade against Hu Shih, he tells us that Hui-neng's great significance in the history of Zen, perhaps to the extent that Zen does actually start with him, is that Hui-neng was the first to equate prajñā with dhyāna. In other words, dhyāna is not just about sitting there and letting your mind go still. It is also about the wisdom you have when are just sitting there. Is dhyāna by this account then still the same as sitcháin? Maybe not. Hui-neng will say that dhyāna is prajñā. Sister Fidelma will ask what "prajñā" means, and the whole paraphernalia of Buddhist discourse will roll into action to explain. Even if Hui-neng were to go into koan mode and say something unrelated, this too would need to be explained. (Fidelma: "You are changing the conversation." Hui-neng: "No, I'm not. I'm doing a koan." Fidelma: "Oh! What's a koan?") There is no getting away from the fact that linking dhyāna to prajñā is to give Zen a philosophy and religion. Of course, Suzuki can claim that this "philosophy" or "religion" is merely the secondary, historically contingent and not really needed explanation of something that is just there regardless of explanation. And so the wheel of ahistorical historicity turns again. Zen is everything because Zen is nothing, but Zen is something. And on it goes.

Zen's Ideological Confusions

The source of Zen's ideological confusions is Suzuki's claim that Zen "abhors media, even the intellectual medium; it is primarily and ultimately a discipline and an experience, which is dependent on no explanation; for an explanation wastes time and energy and is never to the point; all that you get out of it is a misunderstanding and a twisted view of the thing."[62] A media implies that something is representing something else. This means immediately that that which is being represented is not the same as that which is doing the representing. To use one of Suzuki's favorite metaphors, the finger that points at the moon is not the same as the moon. This metaphorical point should be obvious to everyone and yet we go through the world having the world and all that is within it represented to us by secondary signs and signifiers. We rarely see that signifier and signified are separate, that the world is being expressed to us in a way that is not absolute but contingent in the sense that we could be seeing it through other signs, other representations, other understandings. The problem with the finger and the moon is the fact that any finger can point at the moon. If it were just one finger always pointing at the moon then that finger would be, in effect, part of the moon and there would be no signifier and signified divide. But it is that fact that your finger, my finger, that person over there's finger can point at the moon that will mean that there will never be the one finger to represent the moon. Moon and finger will always be an accidental and hence not fully true connection. Sure, we are talking only about the moon and pointing fingers. But let's understand truth and values through this metaphor. Truth represents itself to me through my specific signified beliefs. These will never be the exact same as yours. Does that mean I am right and you are wrong (only my finger points at the moon), or both of us are right (in which case the moon is irrelevant, all we have to go by are fingers).

There is an innate disconnect between our beliefs and the world about which we have those beliefs (the finger is not the moon). But this disconnect is always hidden from us thanks to the merciful functioning of ideology. Ideology provides us with consistent beliefs that act as filters to let us see the world coherently, even when that same ideology tells us that the world is not at all coherent. The notion that those beliefs that an ideology provides are contingent, accidental, have a history, and could be another set of beliefs just the same (all fingers point at the moon) is a serious problem for every ideology. The goal of all ideologies is to have no media. One strategy for doing this is to ground beliefs in ultimate experience of the world. Our beliefs come from our observations of reality just as it is in that form which is just complete obvious common sense.

Reality as Experienced

And so ideologies base their beliefs on empirical data. Look at the example of Marxism which sees its beliefs as following from praxis. History just happens as it does due to the mechanics of materialist dialectics where a particular way of life comes to an end, not because people have better beliefs in their heads, but because that way of life was simply impossible. We live in liberal democracies and not feudalist societies, not because we came up with better beliefs but because of past mass agitation and action that just sprung up as feudalism began to fail. The Marxist interpretation of the world is as objective, empirical, and untheoretical as that. Similarly, positivism, perhaps today's dominant ideology, the idea that rational understandings of our material world will let us constantly improve it, is based on empirical evidence. We see that nature behaves consistently, according to natural laws, and through science we can learn those laws and apply them. We can send rockets to the moon and have them return safely without being zapped by the magic spells of moon goddesses.

So too Zen is empirical. It is actual experience of the sudden awe and absolute knowledge of being here and now that you, me, Suzuki, and my friend Liam (see previous chapter) have experienced with varying intensities. It is an experience that just happens. All empiricism, no theory. The problem, though, is that experience means nothing (literally) without interpretation, and when we interpret we follow always the whispers of our inner ideology. The mass shift from feudalism to capitalism did happen, but it takes ideological interpretation to see this as more than simple random historical events. Similarly, the consistency to be found in nature and its science needs to be interpreted to reach the full-blown cosmology of modern materialism. Hunter-gatherer tribes were far more aware in an everyday way of the cold, cruel, mechanical, and methodical ways of rational nature compared to us cossetted and closeted moderns. They would not have survived otherwise. And yet they also saw spirits, ghost, goblins, and gods in nature, not just the iron laws of materialist naturalism which we only see. So too with Zen. We suddenly know and experience the here and now. But what is this experience? Is it Celtic Christian (and pagan) sitcháin, or is it Buddhist (and Hindu) moksha? Suzuki will tell us it is moksha (satori). And with this he will have given it a shape and form and, most importantly, a *name*. And this name will have attached to it all the content and color and history of his Zen ideology. There is no escape, ever, from the samsara of ideology.

Ideologies as Self-release Traps

While ideologies provide us with our delusions, they can also provide us with an awareness that they are doing this. Marxism has its notions of ideological mystification and false consciousness which it can often turn on itself, sometimes, for example, with the help of hyper-self-reflective psychoanalytic theory. Similarly, positivism never discounts the falsification of its own theories and even methods. Zen ideology, too, is an ideology that is perfectly aware of the ideological nature of all knowledge, including its own knowledge. It does hold out for the possibility of a form of knowledge, that of the here and now, that will always be pure knowledge free of ideological warpings but there is always also the awareness that this pristine knowledge, this infinite wisdom, this unfathomable awareness that is so self-certain that it is beyond all faith, remains in the here and now, centered forever always in where we are at this every moment. But anywhere that is not where this knowledge is at, as in here and now, will immediately again be pulled into the rippling waves of world and subject coming and going as partial and delusional representations of that which is over there beyond us. This can be construed as an argument both for and against Zen ideology. Zen ideology will argue that even with all the partial and impure truths our ideologies fill our consciousness with, there is still always at the very core that part of our consciousness which stands above, beyond, within, over, under (pick your preposition) the fray that remains unchanged and unchained, the prajñā wisdom of the here and now. Most other ideologies do try to ignore, downplay, or eliminate this knowledge of the here and now and focus only on history and nature out there. Not Zen and that is the anti-ideological power of its ideology. The True Person of No Rank can see all other ranks, including his/her/its own, and how false they are.

However, we cannot avoid the other conclusion that when it comes to the ins and outs of social and political issues Zen, in this form, can be dangerously useless. As Suzuki said, it can be wedded to any other ideology, even the not nice ones. This is because it is dealing with a realm of life and human consciousness that simply does not go there. We can talk in the vaguest of terms about how the wisdom of the here and now does connect to the wider values of love and mercy and karuṇā. But in doing so we are still hovering ten thousand miles above the soggy ground of human politicking. Notions of karuṇā will never answer questions such as whether trade unionism is a good thing, or whether liberal democracy is the best political system, or whether austerity is better than quantitative easing. Such questions are far, far away.

Zen, wherever it thrives, does build up its own culture and values that can change over time. The Zen of bushido is vastly different to the Zen to be found today, a Zen that resides comfortably with the liberal values of the pacifist bien-pensant bourgeoisie. The point is that there is "Zen" (the philosophy of prajñā non-dualism) and there is "Zen" (a set of cultural forms that has accidentally emerged in history and is for ever changing). The first Zen, Zen philosophy, should never be beholden to the second Zen, Zen culture. One is the moon, the other is the finger. This is the mistake that Suzuki made when he wrote so lovingly about the samurai and allowed himself to be lured by the false visions of nationalist exclusionism. He had let himself fall for the delusions (avidyā) of his time and place, forgetting the truth of here and now. But note that it is with the philosophy of Zen, the very same that we have learned from Suzuki, that we chastise Suzuki. Let this stand in his favor.

Conclusion

And so Suzuki, who had been so angrily rebuffed by the Zen master Setsumon Rōshi when he had asked intellectual-style questions about Zen all those years ago at Kokutaiji Temple, the first Zen temple he had ever visited, was now many decades later the English-speaking world's foremost intellectual master of Zen, chastising in turn all those who could not fully grasp its philosophy of non-philosophy. One day, a young man with intellectual confusions seeking the solace and wisdom of Zen, just as the younger Suzuki did, came calling suddenly to Suzuki's door. That young man was Jack Kerouac and the meeting took place on the afternoon of October 15, 1958, in New York. Kerouac takes up the story.

> ... Doctor Suzuki made us some green tea, very thick and soupy—he had precisely what idea of what place I should sit, and where my two other friends should sit, the chairs already arranged—he himself sat behind a table and looked at us silently, nodding—I said in a loud voice (because he had told us he was a little deaf) "Why did Bodhidarma come from the West?"—He made no reply—He said, "You three young men sit here quietly & write haikus while I go make some green tea"— He brought us the green tea in cracked old soupbowls of some sort— He told us not forget about the tea—when we left, he pushed us out the door but once we were out on the sidewalk he began giggling at us and pointing his finger and saying "Don't forget the tea!"—I said "I would like to spend the rest of my life with you"—He held up his finger and said "Sometime."[1]

There are parallels between Suzuki's first visit to a Zen temple and Kerouac's visit to Suzuki. In both cases the novice misunderstands how the ready answers of Zen are something it takes time and perseverance to be ready for. Zen, like any philosophy, does have all the answers but you will not get them on your first visit. But also there are differences. Suzuki treated Kerouac with politeness and respect, and while probably seeing Kerouac and his pals as whacked out space cadets, the epitome all that is wrong with decadent dualistic Western civilization, he still humored them and engaged with them. Westerners felt Suzuki had something to say, and Suzuki was happy to say it, even if he believed often it would fall on deaf ears. Suzuki's Zen was a philosophy that spoke to the concerns of a modern society seeking calmness and meaning. Unlike the roshi at Kokutaiji temple, his power came from new ideas rather than old authority.

For many decades Suzuki was widely revered for attempts to reach out and have dialog with the modern world. Many were attracted to Zen from his writings and Zen is now a living religion well beyond the borders of Japan. But in recent decades, Suzuki's legacy has experienced criticism and revision in the works of scholars such as Robert Sharf and Bernard Faure.[2] Some of the criticisms have been well-deserved attacks on Suzuki's wilder nationalist and orientalist assertions (which I will largely agree with shortly) but some of them have implied accusations that Suzuki's Zen is not the real Zen and that Suzuki "invented" a new Zen tradition.

The argument has been that the orthodox Zen of, for example, Setsumon Rōshi who Suzuki first encountered at Kokutaiji Temple is completely different from the Zen Suzuki preached to the West. The general accusation is that existing institutional Zen is about well-defined practice and proper ritual. It is not about an enlightenment experience that suddenly hits you, as Suzuki maintained. However, Victor Hori has disputed these charges pointing out that while Zen temples do follow rituals, they follow these rituals to achieve experiences that are beyond ritual. He argues that "the Zen monastery is a unique institution because it cultivates a nonrational insight through ritual formalism."[3] Furthermore, the sudden experiences of enlightenment that Suzuki described are testified in the Zen literature. Zen satori and the Zen experience, both religiously and sociologically, is as Suzuki described it. He did not make it up.

I would agree with Hori on this. But I would go further and say that while Suzuki did not "invent" a new Zen he did understand it anew in a different way, and that it would have been strange if he had not. The idea that a religion can stay authentic in every way without change, generation in generation out, is a sociological impossibility. People can only understand their religion and inherited beliefs in their own way, which will be shaped socially by who they are and how they live. It is impossible to understand the world through anyone's eyes but your own. Suzuki and Setsumon Roshi at Kokutaiji Temple would have grown up and been educated in vastly different social contexts. Unlike Setsumon Roshi, (I am assuming), Suzuki was exposed to all the new ideas of modernity from birth and would continue to deepen his intake of these as he matured. In understanding Zen, he brought all his learning and education to the task and so, of course, what he had to say was always going to sound different to what the Zen masters of other times would have said. It would have been humanly impossible for him to have done otherwise. Suzuki explained Zen as he knew it, in good faith. There was no invention only teaching, something he did so well that it even brought Jack Kerouac to his door.

But for that teaching to survive and be still respected I think it is necessary to separate within it that which was wise and of value, and that which is a relic of less enlightened times. The top candidate for purging is his concept of Japanese *reisei* (Japanese special spirituality) and his other ideas related to this. I do not think these concepts are fascist or ultranationalist; they are simply incoherent and inutile. They are ideas that Suzuki used to string together random impressions, feelings, and dare we say it, prejudices he had about Japan. It is not hard to do what he did: invent a vague national characteristic and then deploy fragments of history and literature to pretend that it has always been there. Anyone can play this game. I could do the same for Ireland: Looking at spiral rock designs in ancient megalithic tombs, we can say that Ireland has had since ancient times a special *reisei* whereby the world is inscribed in the divine, rather than the divine being inscribed in the world, as in other countries. Christianity merely matured this into a direct awareness of transcendent non-inscribed inscribed divinity, as we can see from later ancient stone Celtic cross engravings. And Irish literature, with the *tariki* inscribed overindulgence of Joyce and the *jiriki* inscribed asceticism of Beckett demonstrates this further. Now, what I have just written is, of course, nonsensical, but it is an imitation discovery of a hidden *reisei* within a nation which, because my descriptions are so incoherent, will be hard to disprove and may be, forgive any immodesty, mistaken for profundity. Which is all to say that there is nothing profound about the idea of *reisei*. Or, indeed, related Suzuki orientalist assertions of an "Eastern Way of Seeing" (東洋的な見方). To save Suzuki's legacy such concepts and ideas need to be junked.

It is Suzuki's other ideas, expressed in even his earliest writings, such as "The Place of Peace in the Heart" (『安心立命の地』, translated in this volume) from 1894, that should be allowed to stand strong and clear. Of value, for example, are Suzuki's assertions about science, that it is a form of knowledge that is perfectly truthful and correct, but which cannot operate within all aspects of reality. Importantly, science cannot explain the "I" experience of consciousness. Various philosophers within contemporary continental philosophy have been making similar arguments, disputing in effect those analytical philosophers and "new atheists" who are convinced that science is equipped to explain absolutely everything absolutely and eventually.[4] As Suzuki points out, science explains more and more each year but it will never get to absolute knowledge no matter how much its knowledge grows.

That science cannot explain everything is not, in fact, a hard argument to win. Indeed, when Richard Dawkins, in exasperation, declares that "the why question is a stupid question," it is a kind of note of surrender and acknowledgment that science will not discover everything.[5] More difficult and more threatening to religion is not the existence of science but, in fact, the existence of other religions. The world is full of different religions, all with their own peculiar supernatural beliefs and irrational rituals. If other faiths look untrue, why should mine be any different? It is a serious challenge to anybody's faith. Suzuki raises the same issue (for example, in his essay "Religion and Science" [宗教と科學] (1949)—translated in this volume), discussing how we have religions, for example, that believe in the rice god Inari (Shinto) or in the Immaculate Conception (Christianity). It is easy to feel that all religions are just products of the human imagine, fantasies that have no bearing on rational material reality. Suzuki's argument was to say that the particular forms of religious belief, the gods and the miracles, are false and superstitious. But religious truth is not based on belief in these; it is based on an actual experience we can all have, and most likely at moments have had, of the here and now—the infinite here and eternal now. This experience which is experienced as absolute knowledge that cannot be unknown, as in the *knowledge that you are here* (try and not know that), cannot be explained or known by science or even rational thinking. Those who forget or do not want to know this experience will have no empathy for religion. Those who do remember and do know it probably will. Either we feel or know or believe it, or we don't. There is no point in beating each other up further about the issue.

But this experience of the here and now, the thusness, the *sonomama*, is also an experience of and in and about and from the absolute emptiness. However, emptiness will always need its form, and here the experience of Zen is a problem. Emptiness is form as the sutras say, but is it any form? Traditionally, it is the form of Zen with all its history, texts, patriarchs, values, beliefs, arts, and culture. But Suzuki holds out the possibility of other forms: those who believe in the rice god Inari or the Immaculate Conception are founding their faith and conviction in the transcendent through the same awareness of the infinite here and eternal now. Indeed, those who practice and experience Zen can even remain, or become, convinced atheists. Japan-based (Soto) Zen practitioner Damien Okado-Gough, for instance, believes that the Zen experience has nothing to do with religion and is compatible with a fully materialist non-religious belief system. He says, "The forms are only of value insofar as they can teach, guide, and support us in the practice of seated meditation. Zazen is a simple, practical exercise. Therefore, religious belief has no role to play in it. After all, Siddhārtha Gautama had nothing but a mind ridden with anxieties and a place to sit."[6] Emptiness is form, but linking the two will always be an aporia for Zen philosophy.

The basic philosophical issues here that Suzuki wrote so much about—the place and truth of science, the experience of emptiness and thusness and its connection to religious belief, the relationship between the cultural world and the absolute nothingness—are all major themes of the Kyoto School over which they pondered throughout the twentieth century. Suzuki's preaching about Zen made it go global. It would be nice if his writings about philosophy were to do the same for the Kyoto School.

The Place of Peace in Our Heart (安心立命の地-1894)

The sky looms over high above us with its deep blueness, the earth spreads out around us into its vastness, stretching out into mountain peaks and the deep of the sea. Between sky and earth are countless creatures: luscious plants and trees, swarming insects, birds fluttering up high, beasts bounding below. There is an almost infinite variety of living things. We know not who creates them or who sorts them. They come and go, born over here, dying over there. Mountains crumble down and become valleys. Seas dry out. Mountains arise. Comets fall and become lumps on the earth. Heat sparks and becomes a star. During the day the sun shines bright lighting up all around. Darkness disappears and brightness takes over, reigns for a while, and then darkness returns. Spring has its budding, summer its flourishing, autumn its harvest, and winter its withering. All moves and changes without confusion in proper order. Who is organizing it all? Who supervises these things? Is there any meaning to it all coming as it does from whither knows? Is there any meaning to it all going as it does to who knows where? You can ask your question to heaven but there will be no answer. You can shout it out to the earth but it will not respond. Our anxieties or sorrows will find no refuge.

What is this creature we call human? On the exterior are eyes, ears, nose, and a mouth. Within are the organs, with a brain at the top and legs provided below. The human stands strong unaided. Are they of the genus of monkeys? Are they descended from the amoeba? Humans boast of being the spirit of creation. When attacked they wail. When gently stroked they feel joy. When it is spring and the days are bright and the flowers bloom, they amble along belong below the blossoms.

When dark autumn comes and the insects chirp, they lean lonely and lugubrious from their windows. Humans are lamentable, obscene, and greedy, wretched of the flesh. But so too do they gather together as companions. Parents discharge their children to the care of teachers filled with charity, devotion, and honesty. And society comes together to protect its orphans. All this is true. Society sees to it that we can go about our business without conflict with others. Which description better fits humans? Are we at either extreme or are we a center of contradiction? What kind of animal are we? We experience pleasure and grief, sadness, and joy. We go through a thousand changes and countless shifts from day to day and from hour to hour, without any stopping. Whatever could equal humans? Did we wander down from heaven? Did we bubble up from the earth? Our eyes and ears will never reveal to us such answers. "What am I?" we ask, but the more we ponder the truth of this wondrous ghost the less becalmed becomes our minds.

The cosmos too is a mystery. This "I" that is I is also a profound conundrum. I do not know what this cosmos is, but more than that, I do not even know what I am. It was Socrates many thousands of years ago who said "We truly do not know." But still we go on in our ignorance, like little boats crossing the wide expanse of ocean with no compass to guide it or instruments to chart its course, with only the odd blasts of breezes from distant horizons on our flimsy white sail to move us. We are not wizards who could control the breeze, nor have we the power to steer our course. The boat sails on without our doing, with no way for us to know where we are headed or where the coastline is. As Hugo lamented, "I do not know where I go, but I still go on." Or as Carlyle said, "The universe was as a mighty Sphinx-riddle, which I know so little of, get must rede or be devoured" (— *Sartor Resartus*).

We are enclosed together, the cosmos and I, in an enormous mysterious storehouse that is forever sealed. We must keep moving without pause or rest, though we do not know where we are. The mystery that reigns over all our minds must be solved for us to find calm. As Emerson wrote, "The instincts presently teach, that the problem of essence must take precedence of all others,—the questions of Whence? What? Whether?"—*Representative men.*

Our anxieties arise from this irresolvable problem. There is no clear answer to give us security. We seek to open the sealed storehouse with a word and attain peace in our hearts (安心立命). We cry out "Open Wheat!" or "Open Barley!" but it is all in vain. If only we just said, "Open Sesame!" It is science that can achieve this opening and will claim the theorists. It is only science that can see the light of the universe, the phenomena of space and time and consciousness through experiences residing in our five senses (all humans are a collection of senses). The myriad of all things are reduced to sixty-three elements. Atoms can be analyzed and the connections between force and material made known. The organization and interactions of everyday complexities are taken apart, their origins discovered, their purity recovered. We can look into the distance, into the darkness with telescopes and instruments for measuring and analysis. We can rise into the sky by lightening the air, we can sink to the depths of the sea in diving bells. We can turn darkness into day with electricity. We can make a thousand miles be near, and steam our way across the ocean waves. We can climb mountains and tear them open with gunpowder and send projectiles flying hundreds of miles.

Long ago, making clouds and calling rain was done by mystic shamans gathering dead leaves in misty and wind battered mountains. Now, the principles of science ensconced in comforts can call forth the thunder and lightning and make rain and wind without going deep into mountains. Those who knew the ways to turn calamity into good fortune were (シソロジカル) theosophical[1] persons, old wise ones carrying a cane, lighting incense, and appearing in half dream states. Whereas it used to be those who were advanced in years who were wise to the ways of the world, now it is our sciences that speculate on the future a billion years hence, and the past a billion years ago with astronomy and geology. We can know the eclipses of the sun and the moon, from whence the winds and rain come, and better ensure good fortune rather than calamity. We can only marvel in wonder at the achievements of science. The fiercest gods are putty in our hands, we crush the heavens underfoot. Nothing can be miraculous in the eyes of science. Everything is simply the interplay of the material and forces and any changes and variations we see in nature are the product of such forces, nothing more. There is nothing beyond our senses and perceptions, to go beyond the empirical is the delusion of madness.

We can only look forward with hope for a new dawn as the world becomes more and more open, and wisdom greater and greater. Ignorance turns to knowledge; darkness turns to light. Such a world without doubts will be as one big machine and the laws of nature will be revealed as it turns. We will attain that place of peace in our hearts (安心立命の地). Only fools will indulge in indecision, hesitation, and hasty faith.

Those who subscribe to this materialist view make science central and talk of how all the things of our world can be understood from our senses and experiences. They see foolish beliefs still stubbornly held by the public to be due to a lack of education. It is good to theorize about that which we want and aim for.

They see us as needing nothing more than science and its benefits with any magic wonder still lingering in the hearts of humans to be of no use. As stones roll and mats unfold, gods are used, power harnessed. Anyone can enwrap their minds in such things. Science believes in the five senses and not intuition. We all must proceed through the gates of speculative reasoning.

Their dogmatic faith is great. "Look!" they say. But are the five senses really to be trusted? Is understanding all the things of this world enough to open the secret storehouse of the universe? They assume that perception arises when there is change, so when there is no change there can be no perception. Without perception there are not the things of this world. For change to occur, there must be discrimination, but discrimination does not allow for equality.

There is the subject and the object, the inside and the outside. This is why discrimination arises. Perception does not arise by simply probing and attacking the external world, but through a harmony with the inner and outer reverberations of the subject and object, without which we would not know the existence of our body nor see the existence of the universe. Scientists look outwards and honor the object, but they forget the subject and do not shine a light inward. This is "Naive Realism"—in other words a shallow and faulty theory. As Mencius said, "All things are prepared within me"[2] or as the Buddhist scriptures say, "All dharmas in one mind," or as Schopenhauer said "Die Welt ist meineVorstellung (The world is my idea"). Sense experience starts in the mind and remains there to the end. Indeed, the essence of the thing evaporates remaining unknown. This is an affront to human nature, leaving the spirit unsatisfied.

Science essentially works on the principle that this is all we have (whether based on sense perception or experience) and that this is simply the world as it is shining into the portals of our five senses, allowing for synthesis, analysis, inferences of causes, and surmising of effects. Science does not question the laws of the physical world (if there are laws or not) and does not seek to investigate the laws at the very bottom of each whole individual human being. They believe in the experience of the senses and reality of the exterior world. But they are never satisfied with this and continue to look and analyze over and over again and cannot secure a "speculative hypothesis." When they seek to explain energy, they penetrate it entirely with sense perception but end up in contradiction, as when they study what exists and what doesn't, what is nothing and what is becoming. But any discerning person can see that this is foolishness. Spencer, a respecter of sense perception, assumed there to be an "unknowable" and sought to open up some means of escape but ended up completely stuck, falling into Humean skepticism. Science even mimics the sophists, forgetting its vocation and in a dogmatic self-justifying manner sees itself, with its sense perception, as unique and beyond criticism.

Either way, they have an eye that is made more discerning through science, and can go closer to knowing themselves. Science deals with the turning world of change and flux (有為有漏　sāsrava), with no power to remove the fetters of the senses. One merely trusts one's own guidance to see this and hear that. The senses are given this duty. Being able to synthesis and analyze the material is due to the power of innate faculties that transcend the experiences of sense perception. To ignore this means we cannot attain the place of peace in the heart where the things of the world withdraw, nor awaken to the mystery of our own self-possession, and quests for spiritual satisfaction will end in confusion and dejection. Materialists say they trust sense perception and do not doubt their experience. They retreat from that which is outside sense perception. Anything which may threaten to transcend experience destroys any argument. Carlyle ridiculed this saying: "Those scientific individuals have been nowhere but where we also are; have seen some handbreadth deeper than we see into the Deep that is infinite, without bottom as without shore."

It is hard to find fulfillment through the sciences of human nature. Opening the secrets of the heavens and proving the mysteries of the inner mind through the sense perception of science is so difficult. Science just shouts "Open Barley!" We must move a step further. One step beyond science is philosophy. Questions come from within the depths of the mind. What of the spirit we have negated that may have been there in the original impressions given to the senses in the substances and forces of objects? The inner mind, while not going too far beyond the conclusions of sense perception, is separate from that perception and is transcendent of experience. It enters into the mysterious and deeper conceptualizations that science casts off. Philosophy is about the study of concepts and looks for a self-conception of the mind, seeking even more for the place of peace in the heart. The unknown "Open Sesame" is another way of describing philosophy.

Philosophy is the study of reason. Reason is peculiar to us humans and that is why Westerners call humans rational creatures. With reason as the priority, there is an inward search for the concept of self, and an outward enquiring into all existing things. Such studies are within the bounds of science, but lead to more profound and noble discoveries. This is perhaps how it is with Plato's Philosopher King and his utopian Republic. However, in ancient times in the west philosophy was not so bound, often mixing with mythology and cosmology. In the Middle Ages, it was the servant of Christianity, functioning as a weapon to defend the dogmas of monasteries. In modern times, it starts to show some independence, although Schleiermacher talks of genuine philosophy being genuine religion, and this does make sense since from a certain perspective both spring forth from deep within the human mind. Both aim to know the essence of the universe and the mind. But there is a great difference between the two and of this we should always be mindful.

Westerners sometimes see religion as synonymous with Christianity. But religion does have a wider scope and includes, among others, Buddhism, Brahmanism, Islam, and Zoroastrianism. Organizationally they are different but here I want to emphasize their common point and contrast this to philosophy. If philosophy or religion were people, philosophy would be a wild mountain ascetic living deep in the mountains. Religion is more like lively and sentimental women and children. The ascetic coolly turns his back on human affairs, sheds all passions, whereas they indulge their emotions. He is like a day in autumn that is harsh and frosty; they are like a day in spring that is mild and sunny. Philosophy is about infiltrating the chaotic world of phenomena armed with only the weapon of reason with which to slice the world apart. Religion is about marching straight into the confused world of human affairs, protected only with the solid shield of non-duality, emitting out the rays of heaven.

One is about solving things, the other is about doing things. The nice thing about religion is that it does not condemn theoretical contradiction. The nice point about philosophy is that it is less condemnatory of immorality. Philosophers' strength is in thinking. Religious people do good deeds, with no regard for speculative thinking.

Religion should not flee theoretical attacks in the name of the sacred. It needs to make its truths firm and solid as a basis to defend against invasion from science and philosophy. In line with this, Pfleidere saw religion as a special feature of life and at the same time a philosophical system, with the essence of religion to be the former and not the latter. To eradicate philosophy and assert supreme ecclesiastical authority through the dogmas of temples without enquiring about anything will invite unintended consequences and not bring satisfaction to people's hearts. After all, philosophy and religion are the reverse sides of each other. Both are one and not one, both are two and not two, philosophy becomes the servant of religion, and tries to become its partner. If we were to outline the difference between the two, it is to ask does the outcome of philosophical learning obtain peace in our hearts.

Philosophy, I feel, does not grant peace of heart. We have reason and reason must not be neglected, must not be obscured, must not be contradicted or made inconsistent. But reason does not fulfill our basic needs. Philosophy is really nothing more than a travel journal. What is a travel journal? It is where the traveler sees some scenery that makes an impression on the mind and then puts pen to paper to describe it, but it is a description and not the actual scenery. A well-written journal can make one feel as though you are stepping into real scenery. But even so it is still a simulation, and being a simulation it does not fulfil totally the human heart. Philosophy is the same. It involves second-hand visions of the universe and derivative images of spirituality, an approach to truth that is simulation. Not everyone has the makings of philosophers and many are like those who mistake a photographic likeness for actual scenery. Philosophers may well confirm for themselves the truth of the universe and awaken to their own spiritual body. But as soon as this is put in writing, crafted into literature, as soon as attempts are made to convey it to others, the truth is lost and it veers from reality, and drifts far away. Reading can be idled learning akin to passing the day playing the flute or listening to bells chime. To explain the universe, Spinoza wrote about "substancia," Leibniz made "monades" his key element, Kant talked of "Ding an sich," Hegel used the "Absolute," Schopenhauer the "Wille," and von Hartmann "Unbewusste." First explain, then refute, and next get more complicated. This side explains, that side talks. Neither sees what the other sees nor gets to stand on shared ground. When something is known an objection is raised. Earth differs from Heaven through its craving for explanations through the guidance of reason. Nobody can ever know the ultimate knowledge.

Knowledge is produced by objects but to trace back to what is pre-object takes masses of conjecture and imagination. We cannot arrange the objects we know without hitting contradictions, inconsistencies, and disarray. I can look and see an object as it is but is it as it is for someone else? It is the same with our different explanations. Feelings will differ between philosophers as faces will differ between people but will be alike. a=a remains an eternal principle.

And so they entrench themselves in their theories, hoping to construct a large enough structure only to have it destroyed by the winds and washed away by the rains. It is built and then soon destroyed. It is here and then gone. Built upon constant troubles. This is the way it is with philosophy east and west. We crave knowledge hoping to sate the utterly hidden dissatisfaction in the human heart with the study of philosophy based on such knowledge. Is there anyone who actually attains full contentment and spiritual relief through this? Let us look and see. As Goethe wrote:

"Habe nun, ach! Philosophie,
Juristerei und Medizin,
Und leider auch Theologie
Durchaus studiert, mit heissem Bemuehn.
Da steh ich nun, ich armer Tor!
Und bin so klug als wie zuvor;
Heisse Magister, heisse Doktor gar
Und ziehe schon an die zehen Jahr
Herauf, herab und quer und krumm
Meine Schueler an der Nase herum-
Und sehe, dass wir nichts wissen koennen!"[3]

What is the point of all this scholarship? We seek peace in our hearts but find only turmoil. We seek faith but are overcome with doubt and confusion. We reach for a fig leaf but get a serpent, losing sight of the divine will. Philosophy is a wolf in sheep's clothing. As Byron lamented:

Philosophy & sciences & the springs
Of wonder, & the wisdom of the world,
O have essayed
But they avail no.

He also wrote:

> That Knowledge is not happiness, & science
> But an exchange of ignorance for that
> Which is another kind of ignorance.

Knowledge becomes quite useless as we reach this point. Whether it be knowledge or reason, when facing peace of heart it must bow and beg apology. We judge reason through reason, we critique knowledge through knowledge. It is like using fire to quench fire or water to stop a flood. I do not wish to argue what is deeper knowledge, let the poems above affirm it. It is not science which seeks to understand the great unfathomable universe and its spirit. It is not philosophy either. How can we attain then these Elysian Fields, this land of milk and honey? Where is the light to lead us out of the wilderness? Who will know the call of "Open Sesame"? We have looked at philosophy and religion and seen how philosophy, which seeks that which religion seeks, fails to find it. So, let us now look to what religion is.

Science and philosophy cannot reveal the secret of the universe or reach the place of peace in our hearts. They have their limits because they prioritize sense perception or base everything on reason. But religion manages to profess the wondrous mystery, cure you of the ills in your heart, and relieve you of your torments. Everyone who seeks it can come to the place of peace in one's heart. This proclamation is not falsehood. Religion has two sides: philosophical (intellectual) and moral (emotional). The value of the former is that it can be argued and discussed within philosophy. But what we need to look at now in earnest is the moral side.

Humans are emotionally fragile and weak-willed. Wherever people live on earth, they need to build temples, shrines, and palaces, their last place of sanctuary. They are places where they can hold festivals for the wild nature they fear, or where they can celebrate the spirits of old heroes, or where they can worship the gods of heaven and earth, or create their images or painted statues of those they idolize, adorning a great edifice that people will devote themselves to and fulfill themselves with throughout their lives with all their hearts and minds. Art flourishes in these places. We have the temple architecture, and prayers engraved upon pictures of gods and buddhas, and garden surroundings. These all show how great is the power of religion, something that can only be known within the deepest recesses of the human mind. When people see that temples such as Asakusa Kanono or Kawazaki Daishi (famous temples in Japan) their confused minds are infiltrated by something. We are confused but the main aim of religion is to penetrate into those vulnerabilities. But when it gets to our weakness, heroic though we may be, we humor the gods like women and children, flatter the buddhas, and pray for happiness in the next world. We are like a starving tiger wagging our tales begging for food. We are deserving of pity.

But we are not just a lump of feelings. Nor do we have only knowledge. Even though we look to knowledge at first, it cannot be just abandoned and cast into the dump. Superficially, science, philosophy, and religion would seem to be separate with their own boundaries. But they are merely three different functions within the one mind. When knowledge, feeling, and meaning reach the extreme they are all united together, and the human mind too unites in fulfillment at this extreme place. As Kant wrote, "In der That is auch reine Vernunft eine so vollkommene Einheit."[4] What I mean is that the human heart becomes complete. To satisfy feeling, we must satisfy knowledge. If knowledge is not satisfied, feeling is not satisfied. One becomes three and three becomes one, the three divisions are combined as one.

But whether combined or separated, religion does prioritize feeling. Is the satisfaction of feeling not the attainment of truth? Feeling does not need the power of knowledge for its satisfaction. This is what pure harmony is. That which is not known cannot be so easily satisfied through the feeling of religion. That is why religion is accessible not just to those with a lively intellect and strong determination, but to little children whose intellect is still growing, or to women with delicate sensitivities, or to frail and aging peasants. Religion encompasses an obscure world removed from knowledge, or which can never absolutely submit to knowledge, as we have already mentioned. But we still we need to make clear the distinction between where knowledge lies and where it doesn't.

At the very least, we must be vigilant as to when knowledge has entered into other jurisdictions. It judges between right and wrong. It divides between black and white. It even takes on the holy name and swaggers around the world of intellect. Knowledge is not forgiving. The sun rises and the hundred ghosts of the night are banished. Knowledge appears and the ten thousand demons tremble in obeisance. We can see in history what knowledge has done to religion. The interpretation of dogma has come to be done scientifically. It has evolved, transformed through the growth of philosophy. The personality and body of God exists objectively through a process of "anthropomorphic" imagination. By knowing the progress of the mystery of the subjective and idealist absolute, religion becomes the slave to knowledge.

The splendid and magnificent and palatial temples and shrines become nothing more than memorials to foolish people. And all those dogmas they teach: believing in one God who created the material world and returning to whom is the goal of human life; or the all compassionate and merciful Amida who embraces us with the Original Vow to save all sentient beings and to whom we must devote ourselves; or the world wherein the Tathagata appears, submission to whom rids us of the conditioned defilements. These are about systemizing desires into trivial rites and rules, enforcing beliefs, restraining free thought. It is all oppressive with lots of restrictions. With regular knowledge, as well as valuing your physical freedom, you can with even more zeal exert your freedom of thought. Mere submission and blind faith is nothing more than the ways of foolish people. Their minds are like wax upon which shapes and images are to be stamped. Their ironstone brains are unmalleable. Their delusions are nothing other than religion.

I am neither advocating nor criticizing with such explanations. I do not crave knowledge so as to attack philosophy, nor do I crave it to criticize religion. It would be a contradiction to do so. Religion is simply to believe. By treating it as knowledge we hand it over to the authority of knowledge. What is excluded from knowledge must depend on the power of faith. But I do not answer that religion is just the teaching of the mysterious and to find peace in one's heart one only has to believe in this mystery. Sure, I hold it as a principle. But if we assert that religion is belief and this belief contradicts knowledge, it is belief, not knowledge, that is to be discarded. Belief transcends knowledge but it must not contradict or conflict with knowledge. Knowledge is really a mechanism to distinguish between right and wrong in faith. When philosophy goes beyond knowledge and tries to assault faith, it is subject to accusations of contradiction. Religion that goes beyond the foundations of faith and tries to attack knowledge falls into the bad ways of delusion. We ought to get rid of knowledge that philosophy cannot deal with, and defend that faith which can be defended through religion. In this way we fulfill both and reach a mediation where we know where we should seek knowledge and where we shouldn't. We should preserve both philosophy and religion and not let one invade the other. We need not be left with just one eye. What do we gain without both?

The situation may seem hopeless at this point. Our dogmas are not enough for us to attain the place of peace in our hearts, not enough to open the great mysterious storehouse of the cosmos. But we must not fear. We are not far from that which lies within the sphinx. Human life is a disappointment from beginning to end. Only a few of us are ever exceptional. But the universe is vast and wide, and human life is a miracle. How can we attain once more our lost Eden? Science can only get to the truths that border sensation. Philosophy only gets as far as the limits of reason. And the truth of religion remains at the boundary of feeling. But they should not be kept to one place and restricted to one situation, otherwise the cosmic mysterious mutual harmony[5] is not possible. Mutual comprehension is impossible with such delays and barriers. At the very extreme it ends in nothing. You ask them to explain but all they can say is confusion. Science has nothing. Philosophy has nothing. Religion has nothing. This is not the peace of heart we should seek. We must seek that which penetrates to the core of the human heart to the very source. When this is reached, the heavens and the

Earth will be alive, the spirit will awake immediately, and bright light will emerge hence to drown out the darkness.

The cosmos is the great profound mystery, but it is nothing more simple than the ordinary way of seeing things. It is like a deaf person not knowing the beauty of music or a blind person being unable to compose calligraphy. It is a matter of having ears or eyes. Seeing the universe or spirituality does not need any special awareness. Those who can look clearly have their eyes and nose straight[6] with nothing strange or miraculous about it. There is nothing mysterious about living nature. We do not need any special vision. The peace in our hearts is just here. This is the "Open Sesame." As Channing said,[7] "We do not perceive Him because he is too near, too inward, too deep to be recognized by our present imperfect consciousness."

Humans are imperfect animals. When we look at things from the distance, we find it hard to judge. When we look up close, it is hard to verify them. The closer we are the harder it is to confirm what something is. And so we find ourselves moving back a distance to look at things and falling into despair. But seeing the truth and finding peace of heart are the easy things to do. But it is also the most difficult. And so, the easy way is to not to go so far, and the hard way is to pass too close. Confucius said, "The way is close, but instead we search for it far." The living cosmos is the closest thing to us. The spiritual is no more than an instant away from us. Science and philosophy, though, are stuck in delusions of the cosmos and the spiritual. In their studies they throw away the living form and look at the shadows. We laugh when we seek a monkey trying to grab the moonlight reflection of a flower in the water. But aren't science and philosophy doing the same foolish thing? We need to lower our sights, intuitively trust the phenomena of our senses. If we do so our mind's eye can intuitively see actual reality. We can know how the things of the world really act. It will shine a light into the bottom of all our confusion and chaos.

Zhuang Zhou writes "as they differ, we see them to be different, (as for instance) the liver and the gall; when we look at them, as they agree, we see them all to be a unity."[8] To calm the human mind is to capture it within this world of creation. Behind the phenomena of the world in which our delusions and obsessions operate[9] there is the immediate oneness of things, where self and object are not two. When this is reached the true face of the universe appears as it is, we do not indulge in our own whims, but our thoughts submerge and we attain the quietness that the human mind desires. We seek contentment in our minds, not suffering. Our minds cannot rest in the world of phenomena. Deep in everyone's hearts there is a will to transcend this and enter the world of mystery which is really the desire to eliminate suffering. Science and philosophy give us knowledge but this does not go beyond the world of things and remains relative. Humans, by nature, seek the absolute and unity, and only with this are they satisfied.

Schopenhauer spoke of the philosophy of consciousness. Scientific consciousness is distant from our actual reality. We do not know the origin of creation. Knowledge teaches of the world of things and teaches about each of these in isolation. And so, it does not seek to peer at the real truth of things. As with the philosophers of ancient India, we should enter into deep thought, leave the external world and return to the self, journey into one's self, search the origins of the mind, and know the secrets of the universe. Do this and there are no troubled sensations and no differentiation. Knowledge cuts up that which is perfection, leaving a messy confusion. If we can return to the self, leave behind all emotions, remove all thoughts, arrive at that place where the senses cannot get preoccupied with things, the ominous dark in-betweenness does not disturb us, the distinctions of time and space fall away, the chain of causality is broken, and we are pervaded by the ten Buddha worlds and a single hair on your head is valued. There will be no place for knowledge to use its power and so we immerse ourselves into the infinite absolute, and directly awaken to it. Through this personal awakening we reach peace in our hearts. Let us listen to the words of Emerson: "The Philosopher said, 'all that he sees, I know,' and the mystic said, 'all that he knows, I see.'"

There is a great difference between seeing and knowing. Seeing means looking at things as they really are. Knowledge is about hearing what is said about them. Those who are born in valleys between mountains cannot see the ocean. They only know about its vastness when they hear about it from others. They will know the seas connect to the sky. They will think that the waves are like high and low peaks. That is what they will think about the great oceans and how they will know them. But one day they will see the ocean and they will be greatly surprised and ask what it is. This is the reality of seeing and hearing in our daily lives. For small things we look and know to judge if it is right or wrong. In the case of our greater destiny, such caution evaporates. Philosophers believe in words and religions believe in dogma. The Yamawaro one-eyed mountain ghost would know as much about the ocean as they do about our greater destiny. Knowledge is closed. To get to the source by which we know what is good or bad, what is right or wrong, and to be able to see into the truth, we must merge with the absolute. Any hope of relief for humans will be through converging with the heavens.

Science, philosophy, and religion are like nothing more than travel journals. We read them but we do not know the actual reality of the landscapes they describe. They will tell us where mountains and lakes are to be found, the arrays of trees and flora, the fluttering and prancing of birds and animals, the great and the small of it all. But these are nothing more than shadows of the real thing. Nothing more than mere bones. We do not know the true wonders of what they are describing. There is no elegance, grace, or sublimity in shadows. No doubt the travelers themselves have experienced the wonders of nature. But what is captured in words is mere dregs and drops. Imagine a scuffle on the roadside and you see people swarming around the scene. You are late to the fray, so you ask people about what they saw. One person will say it was like this, another that it was like that. In other words, everyone will have seen things differently. Even though they have seen the same reality, anyone who questions them will be thrown into great confusion. Reading philosophy is the same experience. Whether it be *nous*, or *sustancia*, or God, or the Absolute, everyone will have their own individual understanding of it.

Each of these philosophical principles entails its own preconceptions and will be studied through a certain bias. This is how truth is arrived at. If you read Spencer it is Spencerian, if you read Lotze it is Lotzian, if you read Kant it is Kantian. We go from one to the other. Each has their own originality but they blind us to the true landscape. A strong youth worthy of the name will push through brambles, struggle through shrubbery, march with courage and scale the summit of Mount Fuji. From there the youth will gaze down on the fields of Japan and stare up at the deep blue sky, and merge with the spiritual energy of the universe. He will gulp in with abandon all the air there in the great expanse of world and firmament. It is when we have struggled up and out like this that we acquire the great faith beyond which peace in the heart is to be found, the place where heaven and earth are inverted. This is the ultimate truth, the ultimate good, the ultimate beauty. When we have reached the ultimate of all things we cannot talk of it to people of knowledge. When we have reached the ends of language and reason, whatever science, philosophy, or religion has to say, will be as petty and useless as twigs and fallen leaves.

Mencius was asked what is "*qi.*" He replied that it was extremely difficult to explain. It is something beyond language. Laozi wrote that the Tao that can be described is not the eternal Tao, the name that can be named is not the eternal name. Confucius said, "Does Heaven ever actually speak? And yet still the four seasons come and go as they do, and all things come into being." You must know it yourself, affirm it yourself in every way, and attain the perfect serenity. The Bible says, "You must be born again." We must exert ourselves to the last. Plato spoke of "philosophical death." Once we are born, we are not satisfied. What is born from the womb is the physical body. It is something asleep, not awoken. When we wake up to this, as a person we cannot be extinguished. The body is a phenomenon. It will eventually be destroyed. Get to the emptiness and void[10] where the relativity of life and death, of coming and going is annihilated. This is where God in Heaven is. This is where the Buddha Lotus is. The adornments of Pure Land, the delights of Eden. As Emerson says, "The readings of philosophy, the creeds of theology, are alike transitory; but the discernment of sacred truth and beauty is perpetual and without essential change."

It is the nature of the eternal path to the eternally unchanging. Thus, in seeing it is to be constant and unchanging. However, if it is abducted by the world of knowledge, or brought to theology or philosophy, the end is contradiction and frustration. It will be subject to the whims of people and be something second hand. If not at the site of the original, the actuality, it will not satisfy the spirit. As Hamlet said, "There are more things in heaven and earth, Horatio, Than are dreamed in your philosophy." The universe is nothing more than sense perception in the imagination of science, nothing more than reasoning in the imagination of philosophy, and nothing more than passion in the imagination of religion. None of the three are awakened to that which is beyond knowledge, or that which is transcended of knowledge in this cosmos, or that which is the source of all the different things of the world. All three of them are like being in the desert with mountains and rivers impossible to grasp as they seem to move further and further into the distance away from you.

When we absorb into our minds the great light of the universe, all things are seen as old friends with nothing strange to us. Everywhere seems like home. Both pessimism and optimism are forgotten. There is no joy or fear about the waves of changes. "Looking serenely at the southern mountain" (in the words of the poet Kobayashi Issa), knowing that the basis of the good life is to be without wanting, letting things come and go.

Looking at all the things in the world we feel confused in our emotions and we cannot get peace of mind. Nothing stops. We become attached to appearances and forget the true things. We do not reflect on the hidden. As I said, there is a difference between knowledge we must crave and knowledge we must not crave. Faith must crave the knowledge that is to be craved. And this knowledge we must crave must be known through the direct intuition of the Tathagata. It is like the three rules of logic. Nobody can doubt that "a=a," thus it cannot be proven further. For that reason it is affirmed. Our knowledge leaves it there, we cannot proceed one step further with it and so therefore we confirm the three basic rules of logic without an ounce of doubt. The place of peace in our hearts is to glimpse for an instant at the light of the Tathagata (or God, or the Absolute—there is no name for it), encountering what is directly there. Belief comes alive from this. "Should even the mountains crumble and the seas dry up" (as the poet Minamoto no Sanetomo says), there is nothing for me to doubt. The basis of great belief must emerge from this. Those who explain with useless dogmas and those who believe them are fools to delusion. Those who do not know the deepest mystery of the mind are fools who dream that science and philosophy can grant peace. It is not wise to create such shallow explanations. Christianity says, "God is alive." But they remove themselves from life itself and then actually wish to hang on to life. They are truly pitiable fools.

I wish now to stop. What I have written is just the dregs of ancient wisdom. Putting another head onto a head makes the wise laugh. For those who have ears, listen to the ancient words of the Buddhist Lin-chi: "Over a mass of reddish flesh there sits a true man who has no title; he is all the time coming in and out from your sense-organs. If you have not yet testified to the fact, Look! Look!"[11]

(『宗教』 [*Religion*] No. 26–28.)

Religion and Science (宗教と科學-1949)

We have been hearing a lot recently about the relationship between science and religion, and belief and theory. There is nothing new about this debate and nothing unusual about seeing it now again. Always implicit in the discussion are the questions of what is religion? What is reason? And how can we face and overcome the contradictions that lie at the heart of human consciousness?

Our everyday lives have been flooded by science and its technologies. We can say that our modern culture is a scientific culture. At the same time, religion has become pressurized by the emergence of science to the extent that its very own existence may be endangered. Science has conquered all of reality and religion must submit to it. Even so, there are those regions where science cannot go and here the field of science is cut off. It is at such conjunctions that disputes arise, and when they do both religion and science will have their own response. Religion is that which is mysterious, so the instinctive scientific response is to ignore it. Science just looks directly at the facts as they are and asks, "What is the reason for this?" When individual religious feeling comes into operation, the scientist, as a genuine scientist, cannot dismiss those feelings outright. Science cannot handle authentic individual desires. They have to be discarded as quickly as possible.

Religion seen objectively is something that emerged in history. But when we look at our own selves and how religion encroaches upon us it piques our minds. It touches, however vaguely, upon the spirituality that prevails everywhere in our lived situation. The scientific minded will say that they are not touched by it. And with this, the dialog between religion and science, between the religious and the scientists will cease and each will assume they have nothing in common with the other. But the religious can see that there is something the scientific have not yet reached. Religious people do not ever reject science. But scientists do often challenge religion and religion is often compelled to respond.

Religion embraces science, but they say that science cannot embrace religion. But when people talk about religion and science they do not always fully understand what we mean by the concept of religion. Similarly, we make the mistake of assuming we can understand the concept, however vaguely, of science. We need to first of all consider somewhat what religion is. Then we can talk about its relationship to science.

Religions present us with various different beliefs: for instance, the belief in Japan in the rice god Inari, or the belief in heaven and hell, or the concrete existence of the soul, or a world between this life and the afterlife. People accept unconditionally the truth of the virgin birth, and the ascension into heaven after the tombstone was rolled away following death. They place their happiness in such beliefs. But these are superstitions. We need to get rid of that which does not accord with today's science. It would be nice if religion stayed within the realms of that which is acceptable to scientific opinion. But religion never does this. However, if we were to get rid of the beliefs I just mentioned, religion would still exist as it does. In fact, it would be made more valid with the shelving of such beliefs.

What does religion look like if it is not to be about belief in the god Inari? We should not seek to give a comprehensive description of beliefs in general. But the substance of religion is that which transcends self-power (自力). Those who worship Inari and build *toriis* (shrine gates) do not question what they believe. It is not even discussed. Self-power cannot chart its own course but it does want to, it must do, and to do so it must have a power that can overcome itself. People will say that Inari is this power and will revere Him to this extent when they pray to Him. Religion is not just this, but either way, whether it be shallow or deep, you yourself alone decide what is possible, whether through reason or through will. Only you can do this. This is the core of religious consciousness. And this is what makes belief in the god Inari a religion.

Many Christians believe in miracles and some say that this is the essence of Christianity. Miracles have always meant a clash with science in the past, and will, indeed, never be rationalized by science in the future either. This means that Christianity contains superstitious elements. But here too we can see the power of religion, something that becomes obvious when we consider why it is that belief in miracles emerges from religion. Miracles are, in fact, human consciousness giving witness to that which exists between heaven and earth and which does not conform to human rationality. People whose sensitivity and way of life have not become completely disconnected with this "irrationality" will seek it in the relative everyday world of experience. And thus we have the "virgin birth," "walking on water," "the resurrection," and all the other miracles. Ultimately, a super-rational realm is not an experience nor actually seen. People who are not equipped with a proper insight into the truth of religious experiences have a tendency to fall into a type of delusion. In fact, they can become even more irrational than that.

Let us also look at belief in heaven and hell in the afterlife. Here too we see religious super-rationality and beliefs that cannot be explained by science. Nobody knows where we go when we die. Nobody has come back from the dead to tell us. Do we have a soul that separates from our bodies to be sent onward to heaven or hell? What is this world of the soul that is separate to the body? Does it have the same laws as this world where our body dwells or are they completely different? Any reports we have of such places just produce all kinds of contradictions that are impossible to take on board. But those who believe in heaven and hell do grasp these and here we can say we have religious belief.

I have to admit that I am a bit flummoxed by the religious quest we see here for the irrational or transcendent. But whether there is a hell or not, we should take religion as a serious experience. The religious life, or what I have termed the world of *spiritual direct awareness* (霊性的直学) is not transcendent in these senses. It is something that must break up the general rational world and build something upon it. Spiritual life is transcendent and thus not irrational. The standpoint of religion starts to develop from that point where rationality has become utterly exhausted. And so we must push rationality to that limit. In other words, religion does not believe that reality is fully covered by reason. However, this does not imply that we recklessly chip away at reason. It is the standpoint which says, "let us reason and talk about that which it does not want to be talked about." Accordingly, religion should always be prepared to listen to the assertions of reason. But it will not agree to the premise that the mechanisms of reason are sufficient to cope fully with reality. Leaving aside the issue of heaven and hell, we can say that dead but living, irrational as it sounds, is the way religion is thinking. Whether it be Buddhist or Christian, there is something general that is transcendental and religious.

This counter-intuitive phrase—living while dead—will seem irrational in the extreme, but it is a declaration made from spiritual direct awareness, and is a declaration that can never be evaluated on the basis of the rational and the sensible. Our senses will tell us that a flower we see is white. Our reason will say that a triangle adds up to a straight angle. And all of these perspectives are each true. The world of spiritual direct awareness has its own word-specific form of expression, where living and dying can indeed be declared to be truly one. Let us return to the question of whether this world of spiritual direct awareness can be excused from the dictates of rationality. What is its relationship to the world of rationality if it cannot be negated rationally? It is here that we see the usual haggling that goes on between science and religion. The problem is not either science or religion but the indirect problem of their relationship to one another. People every day will often say something along the followings lines: "I am so busy each day I do not think about religion," or "If we live a proper life and behave in a regular moral way, this is enough. What religion is there beyond this?"

Religion grows from desires within our own selves. It is not something to be extracted from the outside. Others may forever exhort the merits of religion but if the reaction is not from within the effects of religion will not emerge. Everybody has this inner ability to understand religion. But it is impossible to talk to those who have not passed through her gates. It is like trying to talk to those who are deaf and dumb. Those people who feel that they do not need religion, or do not have the time for religion, are people for whom life outside of the relative, scientific, and social world has no meaning. When we look at the life of grass or trees or cats or dogs, we see a form of life with less needs than us humans. When spring comes, the buds open and the flowers bloom. When it is autumn the fruits are ripe. With winter things whither and wait again for spring. Animals are born with fur to be used in both summer and winter. When they eat or drink, they do not need any cup or bowl. When they sleep, they do not need a bed. They do not seek to build their house nor need any warehousing. They do not store things nor save money. When they fight among themselves, they may bare their teeth, but it is but for a moment and follows the natural laws that shape disputes among rivals in mating. There is no malice intended. They make agreements and do not desire to break them. In other words, they reflect exactly the form that they are. We can see from this that they share none of the problems us humans have.

"We don't have to worry about eating. We don't have to worry about clothes. Morality and social affairs have no concern for us. What is so good exactly about being a human?" This is what plants and animals are thinking. If only we could be the same. Humans envy animals rather than the other way around. "Foxes have dens and birds have nests, but the Son of Man has no place to lay his head." (Matthew 8:20) is the lament of humans. "Consider how the wild flowers grow. They do not labor or spin" (Luke 12:27). It is humans who will covet their clothes. Or to put it another way, the one who does not have to worry about anything other than their daily needs is the one we are to envy. In Ancient China at the time of Emperor Yao, the farmers would say "I dig a well and drink from it, I harvest a field and have food. What has the Emperor's power got to do with me?" Such people are truly imbued with religion. Buddhists too are the like this, living with little burdens as they are in the condition of paradisical salvation (*gokurakuoujou* 極楽往生).

Those who say that religion is only about morality, or that we do not need religion, say so for a multitude of different reasons. I cannot deal with all of them, but I will say that explaining the religion that lies beyond morality to those who see only the morality in religion is like explaining the world of light to those who are blind. We can see morality from religion, but we will not ever see religion from morality. There are also those who will say when asked that, "Morality and religion are merely the functioning of human consciousness, nothing more." But the same people will also allow for the idea that human consciousness has different layers. Here, then, we can say that there is a layer of religious consciousness that everyone has. But to reach it takes patience and wallops of perseverance. Now, by this I do not mean some kind of hidden mysticism. There is nothing hidden to be revealed. It is grandly exposed.[1] But still what cannot be seen, cannot be seen. What lies hidden deep in the clouds cannot be known to you. It takes the grace of God to open the gate of religion.

It may seem that I am saying religion and science have nothing in common to negotiate about but this is not the case. The world of common sense is connected to the world of science. Indeed, science is nothing more than the organization of common sense. For us, common sense is the disorganized accumulation of experiences. Science comes along and systemizes that accumulation, creating concepts to encompass things. It then conducts experiments and observations based on these concepts and aligns any facts that appear with these established concepts. In this way, new concepts are in turn conceived. In fact, science is always about creating new things from new things, so as to acquire a better understanding of our reality. In essence, there is no great difference between science and common sense.

Within the subconscious of those who see themselves as too busy with everyday affairs for religion, and at the bottom of the mind of those who believe that everyday morality is enough for us, there lurks a certain world of knowledge which is no different to common sense. This knowledge, which manifests itself as the essence of science, is built from time and space and theory. It multiplies over time, becoming more accurate, wider, and deeper as it goes along, extending also in space. However, as much as it may do this it never exhausts the ultimate essence of reality. No matter how much this knowledge progresses into the infinite, this situation does not change. This is because such knowledge sees this essence as an object. But what is it that this knowledge is actually knowing about? Whose knowledge is it? Who is it that analyzes experiments, checks out various methods, and conducts minute observations? We know things we did not know, and the secrets of space and time are gradually revealed to us. The progression of scientific consciousness in modern times, in fact, has shortened one hundred years to five or ten years. All sorts of scientific groupings have been set up and scientific research facilities flourish with highly sophisticated research technology and abundant funding. And so, the knowledge us humans have of our natural world, including our very own psychological tendencies, has already greatly diminished and made crude the knowledge of a hundred, or even fifty years ago. How will our image of the world compare to today in ten of twenty years' time? And yet all this knowledge will always be limited. It cannot transcend the infinite.

Science, with its experimentation and observations, enables us to create all sorts of concepts and allows us to explore the very substance of existence. But these concepts are always unperfected, lingering in an in-between state of incompletion. Science is always on an eternal march. Forever it will dwell in a house that still remains under construction. To stop what it does would be its death. A stagnated science is not a science. Science is indeterminate and therefore the world of science, as with science itself, is forever changing its form and nature. The world and reality that science poses as its object is never finally determined or unchanging. We are forever discovering through our experiments and more accurate observations things that were not fully captured by our concepts. We explain things anew, even create new concepts, and our understanding of the reality of objects changes once more. The world of science, like science itself forever shifts its form. Humans observed the sun to be something moving from east to west. The Earth was believed to be something flat continuing on forever. Nobody used to know that air has a weight. When mercury is burned it turns red and that red substance is heavier than the original mercury. It is said that nature hates a vacuum, but it turns out that water cannot be pumped more than thirty-four feet. The world of Newton is not the world of Einstein.

We once believed that light had only seven colors but now we have also infra-red and ultra-violet, and light that penetrates black objects which we can now use as a tool. We can say that the world is never dark now. Consider sound waves: the human ear can hear oscillations within a range of a few thousand. Anything higher or lower does not enter our ears. There have been experiments to show that oscillations of higher than 10,000 can fry an egg. We see these kinds of facts reported all the time in science magazines. The form of the world we know until now changes again, and will change further in ways we do not know. We need new concepts all the time to understand reality. Scientists must always be prepared for this. If not, they will be dancing in out of date clothes. "Superstitions" are those unsold tatters that pile up at the bottom of a draper's drawers.

Scientists see superstition as something religious. But let us not forget the superstitions of science that religion can see. But still, "miracles" cannot be justified scientifically and any superstition in religion should be examined scientifically and reject forthright. They should also be expunged when detected in theoretical thinking and spiritual self-awareness.

We can glimpse here, then, the parley to be had between science and religion. There is a world of science for science and a world of religion for religion. Each of them has its own field but negotiation between them should not be seen as a clash. They are often seen as being incompatible to each other without either adjusting to the other, if such adjustments were ever possible. But both science and religion are human affairs, and as such we can never say that negotiation between them is impossible. Such negative rejections of one another reflects a failure of thinking.

The field of religion is about granting each individual, one by one, peace of mind. This peace of mind cannot be got from science. Science does satisfy our curiosity and thirst for knowledge and to that extent it can give us some peace of mind. But the religious peace of mind is instead something that is complete. It says, "this is it." Scientific satisfaction always adds, "not yet." The field of science is infinite. It continues as it goes. Religion also deals with infinity but it is a different infinity to science. It is infinity as it is. It is not the infinity that moves from one to the next, but that which settles itself in "this here" "this now," looking at the infinite and grasping the infinite. This is how religion brings peace of mind. Science always entails an unsettled mind. We are limited to today's technology and today's facts. What fulfills our knowledge now may change tomorrow. In fact, it always does, and this is the fate of science. It is always looking to the future. The past is only significant in the sense that it is useful for the future. On the other hand, for religion, both the past and the future are seen from the moment of the present. Science is about progress. But religion is about each thought being no thought (念念即無念) which transcends the concept of progress. Science can never experience this "no thought" and "no thought" can never be an object for science.

Scientific research deals with a world that can be tested and observed and harnesses concepts for this. Science just looks at the facts and comprehends concepts to do this, otherwise the facts become disjointed with no chain of association between them. Without this chain there is no knowledge, which is a system that turns on the axis of concepts. However, what is being expressed by a concept will need something to fix it in place, and the production anew of this something is the very life of science. Religion does not give primary importance to the investigation of facts. It tries to understand what is going on beneath these facts and this is its great difference to science. Science's great concern is to pursue each individual thing and create concepts to connect them together. Religion seeks to transcend such concepts. The world of concepts is the world of objects and in such a world the grounds upon which we can stand in inner peace and truth are not to be found there. This world of concepts, a world in construction, is fated to be always seeking its next concept.

The world of religion is the place of creation and uncreation, so it can never satisfy the world of concepts. Religion does use concepts. When these are created from the uncreated they are still dependent on that creation so they do not fully reach that which is uncreated. Religion is about directly grasping that which is uncreated. Where we can clench that which is not bound by the conditions of space and time, that is where we will find religion. And so, therefore, religion cannot be captured by science. We can say that religion does go along with the facts of science. If we think of it in terms of time, science is engaged in tracing one moment after another. Religion, if you like, is focused on the movement in itself of the hand of the clock, a movement that leaves no trace as it is just simply a needle. A clock is made up of gears and coils, and we can change the way the clock is constructed. We can alter the arrangement of the gears inside. We can tweak any of the other conditions we can think of. But the clock must still move if it is to be a clock. Science and the technology of science is happy to play around with the innards of the clock. Religion has no interest in such antics. It just wants the clock to be moving. Science looks to what is outward, religion looks to what is inward.

The world when seen from science is constantly becoming something different. Science's description of the world too is forever changing. The eyes and ears of science see and hear a world today that is not the world of yesterday and will not be the world of tomorrow. With religion it is the opposite. There is no change from past eternity and there will be no change in the future to come. Nowadays we hear a lot about cosmic rays and in ten or twenty years the nature of these rays, as we understand them, will change and our vision of physics will probably change too. But all this is of no concern to the world of religion which is always connected to that which does not change which means that when we think we are talking of something new it is actually not new at all. The world of religion will not change in the slightest in a billion or ten billion years' time. This is the peace of mind of religion.

Believing in the god Inari or in "miracles" is superstition. But such superstitions manifest a "religiousness" that moves at the bottom of such believers' consciousness but whose full expression is impeded. Such full expression can only happen at the place of unmediated knowledge. But once this place is seized, any kind of limited knowledge can attach to it and act as an obstacle. This is the fate of humans, but it is not an unbreakable spell. Rather, it is what gives human existence so much significance and is what we should be grateful for. Religious people know this. Words of gratitude, such as, "praise be," "we are not worthy," and the like, are never to be heard in science.

Religion is thus about feeling something that transcends us humans. Science is always about our limitations and it is this, if anything, that marks the incompatibility between religion and science. We have infinity and we have finitude. It is impossible to conceive of dividing the infinite and the finite. Such talk of division easily gives way to misunderstandings. So let me try and say the following. Religion sees the finite in the infinite and science sees finite only as finite. But even this does not get to the issue. Let us just say that if we are not lacking in the spiritual self-awareness needed to see the infinite in the finite and touch the infinite directly through the finite as it is, we will desire religious sentiment at a superhuman level. Rice god Inari's super-humanness must transfer into humanness for him to be an object for religion. If a superphysical "miracle" is not seen to be a conspicuous event in the physical world the miracle has no religious meaning. We see this in Christianity when Christ on the cross says "My Lord, why have you forsaken me" which was, indeed, a recognition of his humanness. This awareness we have of humanness as divinity is religion. But then after three days. He rises from the tomb, a recognition of his divinity that is superstition. When Christ said, "Lord, why have you forsaken me," He was already manifesting God. This was Him performing the miracle of the resurrection. Seeing death and resurrection simply in terms of the physical body is to stay stuck, I believe, in the realm of superstition. There is death and life in religion. Annihilation and resurrection. That is why it is super-rational and super-natural.

Religion has life and death, but science kills life. This is the great difference between the two. Science analyzes and dissects, weighing things and burning things. Its method is to destroy, not to put together. If when it puts something back together, it is not anymore the living thing. This is the way of science. And in this way science is the world of death. Religion is the world of life. Humans like life and detest death. Even as we die, we wish to live. Many people somehow live and die without knowing religion, but this is human ignorance. Hope is unavoidable for each and every one of us but many do not know this. If we understand this, the world of humans will become immediately a paradise world. When this happens, we will not need religion anymore.

In every religious writings we hear again and again the extortion "Oh ye of little faith!" Or "those of you who have ears, hear!," "those of you who have eyes, see!" All of us have eyes and ears of some form, so why do we have to be called upon to do this. It is because we do not fully use them. Those who dismiss religion and begrudge it are not properly using their eyes and ears. They will claim, "we do have eyes and ears." But they will need to have their earlobes pulled and the dust removed from their eyes to know things for themselves. To wake up to religious consciousness means to turn away from one's parents and cast away all possessions and face persecution in one's life. With this, they will become introspective, departing from the world of senses, intellection, science, and ethics, crying out, "My Lord, why hast thou forsaken me!" This is not resentment of "God," but is the consciousness that starts to flower from reflection on God. Once it begins it will go on to its end. Once awakened, consciousness seeks, for a period, its own fruition and development. Eyes will see, ears will hear, and faith will deepen. This is what those in the world of spiritual direct awakening can tell us. The avocation of religion must be heard through the world of spiritual awakening. I will stop here with this simple, and maybe not very clear, essay that seeks to describe so crudely science and religion.

Notes

Introduction

1   For further details of Suzuki's life, see: A. Irwin Switzer, *D. T. Suzuki: A Biography* (London: The Buddhist Society, 1985). Abe Masao, ed., *A Zen Life: D. T. Suzuki Remembered* (New York; Tokyo: Weatherhill, 1986). Mori Kiyoshi, 『大拙と幾多郎』 [Daisetsu and Kitaro](Tokyo: Asahisensho, 1991). Nishimura Eshin, 『鈴木大拙の原風景』 [Early Days of Suzuki Daisetsu] (Tokyo: Daizoshuppan, 1993). 『鈴木大拙の人と学問』 [Suzuki Daisetsu as person and scholar] (Tokyo: Shunjusha, 2001). Furuta Shōkin, 『鈴木大拙―その人とその思想』 [Suzuki Daisetu—the man and his ideas] (Tokyo: Shunjusha, 1993).

2   For examples of Suzuki's earliest Chinese juvenilia see 『鈴木大拙未公開書簡』 [Unpublished writings of D. T. Suzuki] (Tokyo: Zenbunkakenkyusho, 1989）.

3   『鈴木大拙禅選集10』 「激動期明治の高僧 今北洪川」 [Selected works of Suzuki Daisetsu Volume 10: Wise priest of the turbulent Meiji Era— Imakita Kōsen] (Tokyo: Shunjusha, 2001).

4   For details of the modernization of Buddhism in Japan, see: David L. McMahan, *The Making of Buddhist Modernism* (Oxford; New York: Oxford University Press, 2008). Rick Fields, *How the Swans Came to the Lake* (Boston; London: Shambhala, 1992).

5   Suzuki Daisetu, 『全集第22巻』 「新宗教論」 [Collected works volume 22—A new interpretation of religion]（Tokyo: Iwanamishoten, 1970） For translated excerpts see: D. T. Suzuki, *Selected Works of D. T. Suzuki, Volume III* (California: California University Press, 2016), 3–28.

6   Judith Snodgrass, *Presenting Japanese Buddhism to the West* (Chapel Hill; London: University of North Carolina Press, 2003).

7   Lao-Tze, *The Canon of Reason and Virtue*, trans. Paul Carus and D. T. Suzuki (Chicago; La Salle, IL: Open Court, 1913).

8   D. T. Suzuki, *Outlines of Mahayana Buddhism* (New Delhi: Munshiram Manoharlal, 2007). D. T. Suzuki, *A Brief History of Early Chinese Philosophy* (London: Bibliolife, 1914).

9   For further discussion on Paul Carsus's impact on Suzuki see Margaret H. Dornish, "Aspects of D. T. Suzuki's Early Interpretations of Buddhism and Zen," *The Eastern Buddhist*, 3, no. 1 (1970): 47–66.

10   See, for example, Naito Shiro, *W.B. Yeats's Masks and Plotinus* (Tokyo: Kaibunsha, 1997).

11   『日本的霊性』 [Japanese spirituality] (Tokyo: Iwanamishoten, 1972). It was later translated by Normal Waddel as *Japanese Spirituality* (Tokyo: Yushodo, 1972).

12   Richard DeMartino, "On My First Coming to Meet Dr. D. T. Suzuki," *The Eastern Buddhist*, 2, no. 1 (1967): 69–74.

13   Yamada Yōji 『東京ブギウギと鈴木大拙』 [Tokyo Boogie Woogie and Suzuki Daisetsu] (Tokyo: 東京： Jimbunshoin, 2015).

14   "Editorial," *The Eastern Buddhist*, 2, no. 1 (1967): 1–2.

15   Rupert Gethin, *The Foundations of Buddhism* (Oxford; New York: Oxford University Press, 1998), 19.

16   D. T. Suzuki, "Early Memories," in *Selected Works of D. T. Suzuki, Volume I: Zen* (California: University of California Press, 2015), 204–5.

17   D. T. Suzuki, *Zen Buddhism: Selected Writings of D. T. Suzuki* (New York: Image Books Doubleday, 1956), 260–1.

18   Henry Rosemont, "Is Zen Buddhism a philosophy?" *Philosophy East and West*, 20 (1970): 71–2. [My square brackets]

19   "Remembering Dr. Daisetz T. Suzuki," 150.

20   "Remembering Dr. Daisetz T. Suzuki," 150–1.

21   Hiroshi Sakamoto, "D. T. Suzuki as a Philosopher," *The Eastern Buddhist*, 11, no. 2 (1978): 33.

22   Shimokura Toratarō 『鈴木大拙 禅選集 別巻 （鈴木大拙の人と学問）』 「我々の思想史における大拙博士の位置」 [Suzuki Daisetsu/Zen Selected Works (Suzuki Daisetsu as a person and scholar)—The status of Dr. Daisetsu in our history of thought] (Tokyo: Shunjusha, 1992), 12.

23   Heinrich Dumoulin, *Zen Buddhism in the 20th Century* (New York; Tokyo: Weatherhill, 1992), 8.

24   Kasulis, "The Kyoto School and the West: Review and Evaluation," *The Eastern Buddhist*, 15, no. 2 (1982): 131.

25   William Barrett, "Zen for the West," *Zen Buddhism*, xi.

Chapter 1

1   Mahāyāna Buddhism is one of the three major schools of Buddhism, the other two being Theravāda and Vajrayāna. Mahāyāna, of which Zen is one tradition, is predominant in East Asia, including Japan.

2   Julia Jorati, "Gottfried Leibniz: Philosophy of Mind," *Internet Encyclopedia of Philosophy*, accessed September 10, 2021, https://iep. utm.edu/lei-mind/#H3.

3   *Zen Buddhism and Psychoanalysis,* 1960, 26.

4   The *Lankāvatāra Sutra* is a major sutra in the Mahāyāna tradition that was written originally in Sanskrit and translated into Chinese in the fifth century.

5   *Lankāvatāra Sutra,* 1932, 174.

6   See Benjamin Radcliff and Amy Radcliff, *Understanding Zen* (Boston; Tokyo: Charles E. Tuttle, 1993), 42.

7   *Essays in Zen Buddhism 2,* 2008, 277.

8   Here is Suzuki's go at the same movie-ish metaphor: "By this primary experience which is not logical but issues from a discipline, existence is taken in its truthful signification, all the intellectual scaffoldings and constructions are thus done away with, and what is known as non-discriminative knowledge (*avikalpajñāna*) in Mahayana terminology shines out, and as a result we see that all things are unborn, uncreated, and never pass away, and that all appearances are like magically created figures, or like a dream, like shadows reflected on a screen of eternal solitude and tranquility. The Mahayanist eye is always gazing at the screen itself, but it will be conscious of the screen as long as it is discriminated from the shadows which in turn are themselves discriminations." *Studies in the Lankāvatāra Sutra,* 1930, 295–6.

9   Aśvaghoṣa was an Indian Buddhist philosopher and poet who lived in the first and second centuries AD.

10 *The Awakening of Faith* 1900/2003, 67.

11 *The Rider Encyclopedia of Eastern Philosophy and Religion,* 1986, 7.

12 Suzuki wrote: "The *Ālayavijñāna* is something akin to what may be called the transcendental or universal consciousness which lies behind our ordinary relative empirical consciousness. The purification of this universal consciousness, where all things are conserved in their essence

or in their seed form (*bīja*)—the purification taking place through its individually manifested consciousnesses—is the aim of all Buddhist discipline," *Essays in Zen Buddhism 3* (2008): 340.

13   C.f. pp 55–6, *et passim*.

14   The defilement, as Suzuki explains in a footnote to *The Awakening of the Faith*, (p 80) is of two kinds. One is the natural non-dualistic evolution of the âlaya-vijnâna and the other is ego-specific. They are both separate and so must be annihilated together. The waves disturbing the water disappear most permanently when there is no water. And indeed, *The Awakening Faith* does take its wind and water metaphor to this conclusion: "To illustrate: the water shows the symptoms of disturbance when stirred up by the wind. Have the wind annihilated, and the symptoms of disturbance on the water will also be annihilated, the water itself remaining the same. Let the water itself, however, be annihilated, the symptoms of disturbance would no more be perceptible; because there is nothing there through which it can show itself. Only so long as the water is not annihilated, the symptoms of disturbance may continue." (pp 83–5). Similarly, Suzuki tells us that the great storehouse is not our final goal, cautions us that there are still other metaphors further ahead: "But we must not forget that so long as we are on the psychological plane and referring to the Ālayavijñāna, we are far from the Dharmakāya whose realm is much deeper than our consciousness," *Essays in Zen Buddhism, Third Series* (2008): 340.

15   *Zen in the Art of Archery*, 1953, 6.

16   From *D. T. Suzuki Selected Works 1*. 2016, 12.

17   From *Zen Buddhism: Selected Writings of D. T. Suzuki*, 1956, 238.

18   *Zen Buddhism: Selected Writings of D. T. Suzuki*, 1956, 239–40.

19   *Essays in Zen Buddhism, First Series*, 1949, 21.

20   *Zen Buddhism & Psychoanalysis*, 1960, 62–3.

21   *Studies in the Lankāvatāra Sutra*, 1930, 297.

22   William James, *Psychology: Briefer Course*, 1892, 3.

23   Nishida Kitaro, *An Inquiry into the Good*, 1921/1990.

24   Erich Fromm, *Psychoanalysis and Religion*, 20.

25   Colin Wilson, *The Occult: A History*, 1971, 40.

26   Sigmund Freud, "Dreams and Occultism," *New Introductory Lectures on Psychoanalysis*, 1991, 60–87.

27   Colin Wilson, *C. G. Jung: Lord of the Underworld*, 1984, 116.

28 *An Inquiry into the Good,* 19.
29 Charles Fort, *Lo!,* 1931, 628, accessed August 4, 2021, https://www.sacred-texts.com/fort/lo/index.htm.
30 See D. T. Suzuki, *Swedenborg: Buddha of the North,* 1996.
31 *Zen Buddhism and Psychoanalysis,* 1960, 21–2.
32 *Zen Buddhism and Psychoanalysis,* 22.
33 *The Occult,* 169.
34 『東京ブギウギと鈴木大拙』 [Tokyo Boogie Woogie and Suzuki Daisetsu], 168.
35 Carl Jung, "Foreword," in *An Introduction to Zen Buddhism* (London: Rider and Company, 1949), 27.
36 Jung "Foreword," 156.
37 Jung, "Foreword," 152.
38 Rupert Sheldrake, *Dogs That Know When Their Owners Are Coming Home,* 2011.
39 Eric Fromm, *Psychoanalysis and Religion,* 1950, 96.
40 This can be seen, for example, in the essays "Shin and Zen" and "Sudden and Gradual Enlightenment" in *The Field of Zen.*
41 For further discussion of Fromm's individualist revisions of Freud (and the negative reaction from his erstwhile Frankfurt School comrades) see Stuart Jeffries, *Grand Hotel Abyss* (London; New York: Verso, 2016).
42 Eric Fromm, *To Have or To Be?,* 1976, 19.
43 *Zen and Psychoanalysis,* 55–6.
44 See Slavoj Žižek, *For They Know Not What They Do* (London: New York: Verso, 2002), 9.
45 *Less Than Nothing,* 2012.
46 *Less Than Nothing,* 104 *et passim.*
47 Suzuki, *Zen and Psychoanalysis,* 57.
48 *Field of Zen,* 16.
49 *Field of Zen,* 15.

Chapter 2

1 *Primer of Philosophy,* 1893, 3.
2 *Essays in Zen Buddhism, Third Series,* 133.

3 *Living by Zen,* 80.

4 *Living by Zen,* 80.

5 The expression comes from Dogen. See Izutsu Toshihiko, *Towards a Philosophy of Zen Buddhism,* 27.

6 *Essays in Zen Buddhism, Third Series,* 87.

7 *Zen Buddhism: Selected Writings,* 104.

8 *Zen Buddhism: Selected Writings,* 104.

9 *Zen Buddhism: Selected Writings,* 97.

10 Yamada Shōji, *Shots in the Dark,* 208.

11 Shōji, *Shots in the Dark,* 222.

12 See Alan Watt's obituary of Suzuki: "The 'Mind-less' scholar," *The Eastern Buddhist,* 11, no. 1 (1967): 124–7.

13 For example, Alan W. Watts, *Way of Zen* (London; New York: Penguin Books, 1957).

14 Institutionally, as Leonard points out, "Suzuki was not a true roshi." George J. Leonard, *Into the Light of Things: The Art of the Commonplace from Wordsworth to John Cage* (Chicago: University of Chicago Press, 1994), 154. Note that this is something Suzuki never tried to hide.

15 Christopher Roberts, "Technology Bloggers," October 13, 2014, accessed April 3, http://www.technologybloggers.org/science/the-size-of-space/

16 Albert Low makes a similar distinction between the two types of knowledge: "All of human knowledge is concerned with the *content* of mind. Even physics and chemistry are concerned with the content of mind. Zen is concerned with *mind itself.*" *The Iron Cow of Zen* (Rutland, Vermont; Tokyo: Charles E. Tuttle Company, 1985), 44.

17 *Essays in Zen Buddhism, Second Series,* 93.

18 *Essays in Zen Buddhism, Second Series,* 93.

19 John R. McRae "The Antecedents of Encounter Dialogue in Chinese Ch'an Buddhism," in *The Koan: texts and contexts in Zen Buddhism,* ed. Steven Heine and Dale S. Wright (Oxford; New York: Oxford University Press, 2000), 46.

20 For an example, see Rossa Ó Muireartaigh, "Enlightening Errors: The Case of the Korean Arrow," *Mulberry,* 70 (2020): 31–8..

21 Michael Downing, *Shoes Outside the Door,* 2001, 384.

22 D. T. Suzuki, *The Zen Koan as a Means of Attaining Enlightenment,* 1994, 58.

23 D. T. Suzuki, *The Zen Koan as a Means of Attaining Enlightenment,* 1994, 93.

24 This was C.S. Peirce's point. See Dinda L. Gorlée, *Semiotics and the Problem of Translation* (Amsterdam; Atlanta, GA: 1994), 42 *et passim*.

25 Fukuzawa Yukichi, *An Outline of a Theory of Civilization*, 118. [My square brackets]

26 See, for example, his views on science in the two essays included in this volume.

27 *Essays in Zen Buddhism, First Series*, 315.

28 *Essays in Zen Buddhism, First Series*, 135.

29 See David K. Clark and Norman L. Geizler, *Apologetics in the New Age*, 34–5.

30 R. C. Zaehner, *Zen, Drugs and Mysticism*, 125.

31 Aldous Huxley, *The Doors of Perception* (np: Audio Partners, 1995), 5.

32 D. T. Suzuki, "Religion and drugs," *The Eastern Buddhist*, 4, no. 2 (1971): 129.

33 "Religion and Drugs," 130.

34 "Religion and Drugs," 125.

35 "Religion and Drugs," 131. [Square brackets in the original]

36 *Essays in Zen Buddhism, First Series*, 151.

37 *Essays in Zen Buddhism, Second Series*, 83.

38 Beatrice Lane Suzuki, "The Bodhisattvas," *Eastern Buddhist*, 1–2 (1921): 138.

39 This was, for example, Keiji Nishitani's take on modernity's malaise. See Keiji Nishitani, *The Self-Overcoming of Nihilism* (Albany, NY: State University of New York, 1990).

40 *Living by Zen*, 123.

41 See Nishitani Keiji "Remembering Dr. Daisetz T. Suzuki."

42 Tanabe Hajime, "Requesting the Guidance of Professor Nishida," 2000, 291.

43 William S. Burroughs and Brion Gysin, *The Third Mind*, 1978, np.

44 Dylan, Bob, *Tarantula* (New York: Scribner, 1966), np.

45 Sharon Willis, "Mistranslation, missed translation: Hélène Cixous' Vivre l'orange," in *Rethinking Translation: Discourse, Subjectivity, Ideology*, ed. Lawrence Venuti (London: Routledge, 1992), 107.

46 *Essays in Zen Buddhism, First Series*, 344.

47 *Essays in Zen Buddhism, First Series*, 344.

48 Suzuki Daisetsu 『鈴木大拙全集第 6 巻』 「わが眞宗觀」 [Collected works of D. T. Suzuki—Our Shin Buddhist perspective], 1968, 340. [My translation]

49 Lin-chi, *The Record of Linchi*, 150.

50 Izutsu, *Towards a Philosophy of Zen*, 53–4.

51 Izutsu, *Towards a Philosophy of Zen*, 53–4.

52 Lin-chi, *The Zen Teachings of Master Lin-Chi*, 13.

53 『臨済の基本思想』 [Basic thought of Lin-chi], 424. [My translation]

54 『臨済の基本思想』 [Basic thought of Lin-chi], 424–5. [My translation]

55 『金剛経の禅』 [Diamond Sutra Zen], 105–6. [My translation]

56 *The Lotus and the Robot*, 212.

57 "A Reply from D. T. Suzuki," 56.

58 *The Lotus and the Robot*, 259–60.

59 "A Reply from D. T. Suzuki," 57.

60 *The Lotus and the Robot*, 243.

61 Koestler, *The Act of Creation*, 44.

Chapter 3

1   *Zen in Japanese Culture*, 274.

2   *Zen in Japanese Culture*, 219.

3   *Zen in Japanese Culture*, 273.

4   *Zen in Japanese Culture*, 273.

5   *Zen in Japanese Culture, et passim.*

6   *Zen in Japanese Culture*, 257.

7   Stefan Grace interestingly hints that the book was part of Suzuki's role in presenting a more positive image of Japan to the English-speaking world at the time. See Stefan Grace, "The political context of D. T. Suzuki's early life," *The Eastern Buddhist*, 47, no. 2 (2016): 85 and *et passim*.

8   *The Book of Tea*, 4. [My square brackets].

9   *Zen Buddhism and Its Influence on Japanese Culture*, 45.

10 *Zen Buddhism and Its Influence on Japanese Culture*, 64–5.

11 *Zen at War*, 65.

12 For example, Hagiwara Takao, "Japan and the West in D. T. Suzuki's Nostalgic Double Journeys." *The Eastern Buddhist*, 33, no. 2 (2001): 129–51.

13 Koga Noburu 『鈴木大拙全集第3巻』 （月報6） 「終戦と鈴木大拙先生」 [Collected works of D. T. Suzuki volume 3 (monthly bulletin)—The end of the war and Professor Suzuki](Tokyo: Iwanamishoten), 2000.

14 Cited in Victoria, *Zen at War,* 150.

15 *Zen and Japanese Buddhism,* 3.

16 *Zen and Japanese Buddhism,* 62.

17 D. T. Suzuki, *Manual of Zen Buddhism,* 127–8.

18 Bernard Faure, *Chan Insights and Oversights* (Princeton: Princeton University Press, 1993), 58.

19 See Robert M. Prisig, *Zen and the Art of Motorcycle Maintenance* (1974); David Brandon, *Zen in the Art of Helping* (1991) (about social work); and Jon Sandifer, *Zen and the Art of Cooking* (2001). The book on Zen in the art of outer drainpipe lamination, alas, is yet to be written.

20 Ruth Fuller Sasaki (1892–1967), the erstwhile grande dame of Zen in the west, lamented this paradox in a 1960 book. "Today, due in large part to D. T. Suzuki's voluminous writings in English on Zen … Zen is known *about* in almost every part of the civilized world … Zen is invoked to substantiate the validity of the latest theories in psychology, psychotherapy, philosophy, semantics, mysticism, free-thinking, and what-have-you. It is the magic password at smart cocktail parties and bohemian get-togethers." Ruth Fuller Sasaki, *Rinzai Zen Study for Foreigners in Japan* (Kyoto: First Zen Institute of America in Japan, 1960), 1–2.

21 *The Essence of Buddhism,* 8.

22 *The Essence of Buddhism,* 8.

23 *The Essence of Buddhism,* 9.

24 *The Essence of Buddhism,* 48.

25 *The Zen Teachings of Master Lin-Chi,* 13.

26 See John Heil, *Philosophy of the Mind* (New York and London: Routledge, 2004), 170 and *et passim.*

27 *The Essence of Buddhism,* 12.

28 *The Essence of Buddhism,* 27.

29 *Living by Zen,* 12.

30 *Living by Zen,* 13.

31 See Rosalind Hursthouse and Glen Pettigrove, "Virtue Ethics", *The Stanford Encyclopedia of Philosophy* (Winter 2018 Edition), accessed September 8, 2021, https://plato.stanford.edu/archives/win2018/entries/ethics-virtue/.

32 *Zen Buddhism,* 234.

33 *Zen Buddhism,* 274.

34 *Zen Buddhism,* 259.

35 *Zen Buddhism,* 259.

36 *Zen in Japanese Culture,* 63.

37 *Zen Buddhism and Psychoanalysis,* 59.

38 *Zen Buddhism and Psychoanalysis,* 69.

39 See, for instance, the various articles reproduced in Suzuki Daisatsu 『東洋的な見方』 [The eastern way of seeing] (Tokyo: Iwanahabunko, 1997).

40 D. T. Suzuki and Okamura Mihoko, "Notes and Fragments." *The Eastern Buddhist,* 33, no. 2 (2001): 1.

41 Slavoj Žižek goes as far as to say that " … Western Buddhism this pop-cultural phenomenon preaching inner distance and indifference towards the frantic pace of free-market competition, is arguably the most efficient way for us to participate fully in the capitalist dynamic, while retaining the appearance of mental sanity—in short, the paradigmatic ideology of late capitalism." *For they do not know what they do,* xliii.

42 *Zen in Japanese Culture,* 145.

43 Žižek, *For They Know Not What They Do,* xlvi.

44 Suzuki Daisetsu 『鈴木大拙全集第19巻』 「文化と宗教」 [The collected works of D. T. Suzuki volume 19—Culture and Religion], 50. [My translation]

45 *Essays in Zen Buddhism, First Series,* 60.

46 *Essays in Zen Buddhism, First Series,* 60.

47 『禅の思想ー鈴木大拙禅選集１』 [Zen thought: Suzuki Daisetsu selected zen works 1].『鈴木大拙全集第3巻』 「臨済の基本思想」 [Collected works of Suzuki Daisetsu Volume 3: Basic thought of Rinzai].

48 *Japanese Spirituality,* 94.

49 *Japanese Spirituality,* 44–5.

50 *Japanese Spirituality,* 100.

51 *Zen in Japanese Culture,* 47.

52 *An Introduction to Zen Buddhism,* 44–5.

53 Shih, Hu, "Ch'an (Zen) Buddhism in China: Its History and Method," *Philosophy East and West,* 3, no. 1 (1953): 3. [My square brackets]

54 "Ch'an (Zen) Buddhism in China: Its History and Method," 3.

55 Suzuki, Daisetz Teitaro, "Zen: A Reply to Hu Shih," *Philosophy East and West,* 3, no. 1 (1953): 25–46.

56 See John R. McRae, "Introduction," in Heinrich Dumoulin, *Zen Buddhism: India and China* (Bloomington, IN: World Wisdom, 2005), xxxvi.

57 "Zen: A Reply to Hu Shih", 42.

58 *Celtic Women*, 175.

59 D. T. Suzuki, *An Introduction to Zen Buddhism* (London: Rider and Company, 1949), 45.

60 See, for example, Dom Aelred Graham, *Zen Catholicism* (New York: Harcourt, Brace & World, 1963).

61 *Mysticism: Christian and Buddhist*, 113.

62 *An Introduction to Zen Buddhism*, 74.

Conclusion

1 Quoted in Rick Field, *How the Swans Came to the Lake*, 223–4.

2 For example, Sharf, Robert H, "The Zen of Japanese Nationalism," 1993. Bernard Faure *Chan Insights and Oversights*, 1993.

3 Hori, Victor Sōgen, "D. T. Suzuki and the Invention of Tradition," *The Eastern Buddhist*, 47, no. 2 (2016): 61.

4 See, for example, Geoff Pfeifer, *The New Materialism: Althusser, Badiou, and Zizek* (New York: Routledge, 2015).

5 See "Richard Dawkins vs. William Lane Craig Debate" (video of debate), accessed April 5, 2021, https://www.youtube.com/watch?v=Uaq6ORDx1C4.

6 Damien Okado-Gough, e-mail message to the author, April 5, 2021.

The Place of Peace in Our Heart

1 Suzuki's word here "シソロジカル" is unclear.

2 Translation by A. Charles Muller, accessed April 5, 2021, http://www.acmuller.net/con-dao/mencius.html.

3 I've studied now Philosophy
And Jurisprudence, Medicine,
And even, alas! Theology

All through and through with ardour keen!
Here now I stand, poor fool, and see
I'm just as wise as formerly.
Am called a Master, even Doctor too,
And now I've nearly ten years through
Pulled my students by their noses to and fro
And up and down, across, about,
And see there's nothing we can know!
Translation by George Madison Priest, accessed April 2, 2020, http://einam.com/faust/index.html.

4   "Indeed, pure reason is also such a perfect unity." Translation by Aongus Murtagh, e-mail message to the author, April 6, 2021.

5   円融自在妙用不可思議, a phrase from the *Avatamsaka Sutra*.

6   眼横鼻直 is a Zen phrase.

7   Suzuki wrote the name in katakana only. I am assuming it to be William Ellery Channing (1780–1842).

8   Translation from "ctext.org," accessed April 2, 2021, https://ctext.org/zhuangzi/seal-of-virtue-complete.

9   The phrase 逐物而迷己 appears in Case 46 of the Zen *Blue Cliff Records*.

10 沖漠無朕, a phrase from the ancient Chinese philosophers Cheng Hao and Cheng Yi.

11 Translation of Lin-chi by Suzuki, *Essays in Zen Buddhism, First Series*. 1949, 21.

Religion and Science

1   This is the Zen phrase 露堂堂.

Bibliography

A Zen Life: D. T. Suzuki Remembered. Edited by Abe Masao. New York; Tokyo: Weatherhill, 1986.

Abe, Masao. *Zen and Western Thought.* Honolulu: University of Hawaii Press, 1985.

Burroughs William S. and Gysin Brion. *The Third Mind.* New York: Viking Press, 1978.

Carus, Paul. *Primer of Philosophy.* Chicago: Open Court, 1893.

Clark, David K, and Normal L. Geisler. *Apologetics in the New Age: A Christian Critique of Pantheism.* Eugene, OR: Wipf and Stock, 1990.

DeMartino, Richard. "On My First Coming to Meet Dr. D. T. Suzuki." *The Eastern Buddhist,* 2, no. 1 (1967): 69–74.

Dornish, Margaret H. "Aspects of D. T. Suzuki's Early Interpretations of Buddhism and Zen." *The Eastern Buddhist,* 3, no. 1 (1970): 47–66.

Downing, Michael. *Shoes Outside the Door: Desire, Devotion, and Excess at San Francisco Zen Centre.* Washington DC: Counterpoint, 2001.

Dumoulin, Heinrich. *Zen Buddhism in the 20th Century.* Translated by Joseph O'Leary. New York; Tokyo: Weatherhill, 1992.

Dumoulin, Heinrich. *Zen Buddhism: A History-India and China.* Bloomington, Indiana: World Wisdom, 2005.

Ellis, Peter Berresford. *Celtic Women: Women in Celtic Society and Literature.* Michigan: William B. Eerdmans Publishing Company Grand Rapids, 1995.

Faure, Bernard. *Chan Insights and Oversights.* Princeton: Princeton University Press, 1993.

Fields, Rick. *How the Swans Came to the Lake.* Boston; London: Shambhala, 1992.

Fort, Charles. *Lo!* Claude New York: Kendall, 1931.

Freud, Sigmund. *New Introductory Lectures on Psychoanalysis.* Harmondsworth: Penguin Books, 1991.

Fromm, Eric. *Psychoanalysis and Religion.* New Haven; London: Yale University Press, 1950.

Fromm, Eric. *To Have or To Be?* New York: Harper and Row, 1976.

Fukuzawa, Yukichi. *An Outline of a Theory of Civilization.* Translated by David A. Dilworth and G. Cameron Hurst III, Tokyo: Keio University Press. 1875/2008.

Gethin, Rupert. *The Foundations of Buddhism*. Oxford; New York: Oxford University Press, 1998.

Gorlée, Dinda L. *Semiotics and the Problem of Translation: With Special Reference to the Semiotics of Charles S. Pierce*. Amsterdam; Atlanta, GA: Rodopi, 1994.

Grace, Stefan. "The Political Context of D. T. Suzuki's Early Life." *The Eastern Buddhist*, 47, no. 2 (2016): 83–99.

Hagiwara, Takao. "Japan and the West in D. T. Suzuki's Nostalgic Double Journeys." *The Eastern Buddhist*, 33, no. 2 (2001): 129–51.

Heine, Steven. *Zen Skin, Zen Marrow: Will the Real Zen Buddhism Please Stand Up?* Oxford: Oxford University Press, 2008.

Hori, Victor Sōgen. "D. T. Suzuki and the Invention of Tradition." *The Eastern Buddhist*, 47, no. 2 (2016): 41–81.

Hu Shi. "Ch'an (Zen) Buddhism in China: Its History and Method." *Philosophy East and West*, 3, no. 1 (April, 1953): 3–24.

Huxley, Aldous. *The Doors Of Perception*. np: Audio Partners, 1995.

Izutsu, Toshihiko. *Towards a Philosophy of Zen Buddhism*. Boulder, CO: Prajñā Press, 1982.

James, William. *The Text Book of Psychology*. London: Macmillan, 1892.

Jung, Carl. Foreword to *An Introduction to Zen Buddhism*. London: Rider and Company, 1949.

Kasulis, Thomas P. "The Kyoto School and the West: Review and Evaluation." *The Eastern Buddhist*, 15, no. 2 (1982): 125–44.

Kasulis, Thomas P. *Zen Action Zen Person*. Honolulu: University of Hawaii Press, 1981.

Koestler, Arthur. *The Act of Creation*. London: Hutchinson, 1964.

Koestler, Arthur. *The Lotus and the Robot*. New York: Harper, 1960.

Koga, Noboru. 『鈴木大拙全集 3 』「終戦と鈴木大拙先生」6 月報 6 ）[Suzuki Daisetsu collected works, volume 3: The End of the War and Professor Suzuki (Monthly Bulletin 6)] Iwanami Shoten, 2000.

Lao-Tze. *The Canon of Reason and Virtue*. Translated by Paul Carus and D. T. Suzuki. Chicago; La Salle, IL: Open Court, 1913.

Leonard, George J. *Into the Light of Things: The Art of the Commonplace from Wordsworth to John Cage*. Chicago; London: University of Chicago Press, 1994.

Lin-chi. *The Zen Teachings of Master Lin-Chi*. Translation by Burton Watson. New York: Columbia University Press, 1999.

Low, Albert. *The Iron Cow of Zen*. Rutland, VT; Tokyo: Charles E. Tuttle Company, 1985.

McMahan, David L. *The Making of Buddhist Modernism*. Oxford; New York: Oxford University Press, 2008.

McRae, John R. *Seeing through Zen: Encounter, Transformation, and Genealogy in Chinese Chan Buddhism*. Berkeley; Los Angeles: University of California Press, 2003.

McRae, John R. "The Antecedents of Encounter Dialogue in Chinese Ch'an Buddhism." In *The Koan: Texts and Contexts in Zen Buddhism*. Edited by Steven Heine and Dale S. Wright. Oxford; New York: Oxford University Press, 2000.

Mori, Kiyoshi. 『大拙と幾多郎』 [Daisetsu and Kitaro]. Tokyo: Asahisensho,1991.

Naito, Shiro. *W.B. Yeats's Masks and Plotinus*. Tokyo: Kaibunsha, 1997.

Nishimura, Eshin. 『鈴木大拙の原風景』 [Suzuki Daisetsu's Early Memories]. Tokyo: Daizoshuppan, 1993.

Nishitani, Keiji. "Remembering Dr. Daisetz T. Suzuki." In *A Zen Life: D. T. Suzuki Remembered*. Edited by Masao Abe. New York; Tokyo: Weatherhill, 1986.

Nishitani, Keiji. *The Self-Overcoming of Nihilism*. Translated by Graham Parkes and Setsuko Aihara. Albany, NY: State University of New York, 1990.

Ó Muireartaigh, Rossa. "Enlightening Errors: The Case of the Korean Arrow." *Mulberry*, 70 (2020): 31–8.

Okakura, Kakuzo. *The Book of Tea*. Tokyo: Kenkyusha, 1939.

Pfeifer, Geoff. *The New Materialism: Althusser, Badiou, and Zizek*. New York: Routledge, 2015.

Radcliff, Benjamin and Amy Radcliff. *Understanding Zen*. Boston; Tokyo: Charles E. Tuttle, 1993.

Rosemont, Henry. "Is Zen Buddhism a Philosophy?" *Philosophy East and West*, 20 (1970): 63–72.

Sakamoto, Hiroshi. "D. T. Suzuki as a Philosopher." *The Eastern Buddhist*, 11, no. 2 (1978): 33–42.

Sharf, Robert H. "The Zen of Japanese Nationalism." *History of Religions*, 33, no. 1 (1993): 1–43. Accessed April 5, 2021. http://www.jstor.org/stable/1062782.

Sheldrake, Rupert. *Dogs That Know When Their Owners Are Coming Home*. New York: Crown, 2011.

Snodgrass, Judith *Presenting Japanese Buddhism to the West*. Chapel Hill; London: University of North Carolina Press, 2003.

Suzuki, Beatrice Lane. "The Bodhisattvas." *The Eastern Buddhist*, 1–2 (1921): 131–9.

Suzuki, D. T. *A Brief History of Early Chinese Philosophy*. London: Probsthai, 1914.

Suzuki, D. T. *Essays in Zen Buddhism, First Series*. New York: Grove Press, 1927/1949.

Suzuki, D. T. *Essays in Zen Buddhism, Second Series*. New Delhi: Munshiram Manoharial, 1933/2008.

Suzuki, D. T. *Essays in Zen Buddhism, Third Series*. New Delhi: Munshiram Manoharlal, 1934/2008.

Suzuki, D. T. *The Essence of Buddhism*. London: Buddhist Society, 1947.

Suzuki, D. T. *Living by Zen: A Synthesis of the Historical and Practical Aspects of Zen Buddhism*. York Beach, ME: Samuel Weiser, Inc., 1950.

Suzuki, D. T. "Zen: A Reply to Hu Shih." *Philosophy East and West*, 3, no. 1 (April, 1953): 25–46.

Suzuki, D. T. *Zen Buddhism: Selected Writings of D. T. Suzuki*. Edited by William Barrett. New York: Image Books Doubleday, 1956.

Suzuki, D. T. *Mysticism: Christian and Buddhist*. London; New York: Routledge, 1957.

Suzuki, D. T. *Zen and Japanese Buddhism*. Tokyo: Japan Travel Bureau, 1958.

Suzuki, D. T. *Zen and Japanese Culture*. Tokyo: Charles Tuttle Company, 1959.

Suzuki, D. T. "Religion and Drugs." *The Eastern Buddhist*, 4, no. 2 (1971): 128–33.

Suzuki, D. T. *Japanese Spirituality*. Translated by Norman Waddell. Tokyo: Japan Society for the Promotion of Science, 1972.

Suzuki, D. T. *The Field of Zen*. London: The Buddhist Society, 1980.

Suzuki, D. T. *The Zen Koan as a Means of Attaining Enlightenment*. Boston; Tokyo: Charles E. Tuttle, 1994.

Suzuki, D. T. *Swedenborg: Buddha of the North*. Translated by Andrew Bernstein. West Chester, PA: Swedenborg Foundation, 1996.

Suzuki, D. T. *Outlines of Mahayana Buddhism*. New Delhi: Munshiram Manoharlal, 2007.

Suzuki, D. T. *Selected Works of D. T. Suzuki, Volume I: Zen*. Oakland, CA: University of California Press, 2015, 204–5.

Suzuki, D. T. *Selected Works of D. T. Suzuki, Volume III: Comparative Religion*. Edited by Jeff Wilson and Tomoe Moriya. Oakland, CA: University of California Press, 2016.

Suzuki, D. T. *Manual of Zen Buddhism*. New York: Grove Press, 1969.

Suzuki, D. T., Erich Fromm, and Richard DeMartino. *Zen Buddhism and Psychoanalysis.* London: George Allen and Unwin, 1960.

Switzer, A. Irwin. *D. T. Suzuki: A Biography.* London: The Buddhist Society, 1985.

Tanabe Hajime "Requesting the Guidance of Professor Nishida." Translation by Richard Stone, *Asian Philosophical Texts: Exploring Hidden Sources.* Edited by Takeshi Morisato and Roman Paşca. Milan: Mimesis International, 1930/2020.

Tanabe, Hajime. *Philosophy as Metanoetics.* Translated by Yoshinori Takeuchi, Valdo Viglielmo and James W. Heisig. Nagoya: Chisokuda, 1986/2016.

The Record of Linji. Translated by Ruth Fuller Sasaki. Honolulu: University of Hawai'i Press, 2008.

Victoria, Brian. *Zen at War.* New York; Tokyo: Weatherhill, 1997.

Watts, Alan. *The Way of Zen.* London; New York: Penguin Books, 1957.

Willis, Sharon. "Mistranslation, Missed Translation: Hélène Cixous' Vivre l'orange." *Rethinking Translation: Discourse, Subjectivity, Ideology.* Edited by Lawrence Venuti. London; New York: Routledge, 1992.

Wilson, Colin. *C. G. Jung: Lord of the Underworld.* Wellingborough, Northamptonshire: The Aquarian Press, 1984.

Wilson, Colin. *The Occult: A History.* New York: Random House, 1971.

Wright, Dale S. *Philosophical Meditations on Zen Buddhism.* Cambridge: Cambridge University Press, 1998.

Yamada, Shoji. *Shots in the Dark: Japan, Zen, and the West.* Translated by Earl Hartman. Chicago; London: University of Chicago Press, 2009.

Yamada, Shoji. 『東京ブギウギと鈴木大拙』 [Tokyo Boogie Woogie and Suzuki Daisetsu]. Tokyo: Jimbun Shoin, 2015.

Zaehner, R.C. *Zen, Drugs and Mysticism.* New York: Pantheon Books, 1972.

Žižek, Slavoj. *Less Than Nothing: Hegel and the Shadow of Dialectical Materialism.* London; New York: Verso, 2012.

Žižek, Slavoj. *For They Know Not What They Do: Enjoyment as a Political Factor.* London; New York: Verso, 1991.

『鈴木大拙の人と学問』 [Suzuki Daisetsu as person and scholar]. Tokyo: Shunjusha, 2001

『鈴木大拙全集第1–40巻』 [Suzuki Daisetsu Collected Works Volumes 1–40]. Tokyo: Shunjusha, 2002.

『鈴木大拙禅選集1–11巻、別巻』[Suzuki Daisetsu selected zen works volumes 1–11 and supplementary volume]. Tokyo: Shunjusha, 2001.

『鈴木大拙未公開書簡』[Unpublished writings of D. T. Suzuki] Tokyo: The Institute for Zen Studies, 1989.

Index